101 Prayers for

Let's Begin
With a

Prayer

Sally Macke

Liguori
LIGUORI, MISSOURI

Acknowledgments

I am grateful to Mercy Health for allowing me to use their "Practical Tips for Leading Prayer" from the *Mercy Book of Prayers*. Mercy uses these "Practical Tips" to orient new leaders on how to lead prayer. A special thank you for the support of Mercy's East Regional Director of Pastoral Services Kenneth Potzman; Julie Jones, executive director of Mission and Ministry; and Brian O'Toole, senior vice president of Mission and Ethics.

✦✦✦✦

Imprimi Potest:
Harry Grile, CSsR, Provincial
Denver Province, The Redemptorists

Published by Liguori Publications
Liguori, Missouri 63057

To order, visit Liguori.org or call 800-325-9521.

Library of Congress Cataloging-in-Publication Data

Macke, Sally.
  Let's begin with a prayer : 101 prayers for meetings / Sally Macke.—First Edition.
    pages cm
  ISBN 978-0-7648-2212-4
  1. Prayers. 2. Meetings—Miscellanea. I. Title.
  BV245.M17 2014
  264'.13—dc23
                        2014018799
p ISBN 978-0-7648-2212-4
e ISBN 978-0-7648-6888-7

Scripture quotations are from *New Revised Standard Version Bible,* copyright © 1989 National Council of the Churches of Christ in the United States of America. Used by permission. All rights reserved.

Liguori Publications, a nonprofit corporation, is an apostolate of the Redemptorists. To learn more about the Redemptorists, visit Redemptorists.com.

Printed in the United States of America
18 17 16 15 14 / 5 4 3 2 1
First Edition

Contents

Prayers for God's People

Celebrating the Saints and Holy People

Celebrating Liturgical Seasons

Advent

Christmas

Lent

Easter

Celebrating Special Days

Feast Days

Holidays

Prayers for Following Jesus

Theological Virtues

Cardinal Virtues

Gifts of the Holy Spirit

Introduction

Let's Begin With a Prayer is for use by faith-based institutions that periodically gather for any reason. The goal of any faith-based organization is to further the mission of Jesus Christ: feed the hungry, welcome the stranger, clothe the naked, give shelter to the homeless, heal the sick. As the scope of Jesus' mission is so broad, so are the themes of our prayers. They have been written to fit any number of occasions in which people are working together to build up the kingdom of God. Our hope is that these prayers will help foster relationships between those who are using their gifts to help others, and that together, they will feel guided by the Spirit as they follow Jesus' call.

Jesus prayed often during his life, and Scripture shows us that prayer was important to his ministry. As people who are called to work together to further Jesus' mission, we can be mindful that prayer is the glue that binds us all together. It is an expression of our belief that we are doing God's work to the best of our ability. Our shared, communal prayer is perhaps the most important thing we do to make sure that everything we do is inspired by and guided by God. The practice of praying before meetings in any faith-based institution reflects the focus on our relationships with one another as grounded in our relationship between us and God.

Prayer is something we all can do. Prayer grounds us; it sets the tone for our work and reminds us that we aren't in this work of ministry by ourselves or for ourselves. When we ask God for guidance and wisdom, for help with our needs as well as the needs of others, when we open ourselves to God's love and compassion, we become changed. We become more loving people ourselves. We become strengthened and empowered to do the work we are called to do.

How to Use This Book

These prayers were written to be used before meetings or for any event for which prayer is appropriate. I have tried to create prayers that fit a variety of contexts within our lives of ministry. They are meant to be read aloud, either by the leader of the group or by individual members of that group.

The table of contents can be used to help select the appropriate prayer for a particular meeting. "Prayers for Everyday Occasions" reflects some of the many situations we encounter as we attempt to do God's work. "Prayers for God's People" can be used to lift up a variety of persons in the body of Christ. The prayers in "Celebrating the Saints and Holy People" can be used on the feast days of the various saints included. Prayers to mark the liturgical seasons of Advent, Christmas, Lent, and Easter—as well as various feast days (which include a few solemnities) and secular holidays—have been written to assist ministers praying on those occasions. Finally, "Prayers for Following Jesus" includes prayers reflecting the theological and cardinal virtues as well as the gifts of the Holy Spirit. They have been prepared to help us stay focused in our lives of faith.

Practical Tips
for Leading Prayer

Here are some practical tips that may help you when leading prayer:

✝ *Settle yourself.* When getting ready to lead prayer, ask for a moment of silence within the group you are about to lead.

✝ *Call to prayer.* Invite the group to pray, identifying the purpose for coming together.

✝ *Set the tone and create stillness.* This can be a challenge when your prayer is in the middle of a busy workday.

✝ *Pace is important.* Speak slowly, distinctly, and deliberately.

✝ *Use tone and inflection.* It is important to speak with conviction to hold participants' interest.

✝ *Be patient and spontaneous.* As appropriate, invite the group to pray, and give them a moment to collect their thoughts.

✝ Finally, *close with a pause.* This provides a moment to reflect before returning to the busy day.

Prayers for Everyday Occasions

For Collaboration

Now there are varieties of gifts, but the same Spirit;
and there are varieties of services, but the same Lord;
and there are varieties of activities, but it is the same God
who activates all of them in everyone.

1 Corinthians 12:4–6

Meditation: Are we willing to use our gifts for the good of our community (department, organization, church, hospital, etc.)? Likewise, are we open to others using their gifts for the good of all? We can accomplish much more together than we can on our own. The story of stone soup, in which a group of villagers each contribute whatever food they have to make a delicious soup for all, illustrates this point.

Prayer: Loving God, we thank you for bringing us together in this place at this time. We thank you for your love that inspires us to give of ourselves in the ways you have called each of us to give.

We know that, together, we are invited to be your hands and your feet in a world that sorely needs your help. We ask for the grace to use our gifts wisely in the service of your kingdom.

Each of us is gifted differently, yet we are all created in your image, and we marvel at your foresight in making each person distinct, yet part of a wonderful whole. We ask you to bless our work together and to make us ever mindful that, without you, we are nothing.

Store in us a vision of the good we can create collectively. May we never lose sight of our true purpose, which is to be your instruments of love here on earth.

Be a safety net for us on the days we stumble and fall. Give us the wisdom to look to you for courage and strength, and energy for the times when we are tired.

We are honored you have chosen us to do your work, and we ask that we may always cherish the responsibility you have given us. We pray all these things in the name of Jesus. Amen.

Finding Joy
in the Small Moments

Therefore my heart is glad, and my soul rejoices; my body also rests secure. You show me the path of life. In your presence there is fullness of joy; in your right hand are pleasures forevermore.

Psalm 16:9, 11

Meditation: In the midst of our busy days of work, it is important to cultivate an "attitude of gratitude" that enables us to find joy in the small moments. The smile of a coworker, a steaming cup of coffee, the pretty view outside a window—these can all serve to foster a sense of contentment that seeks and finds the positive in the mundane events of every day. Finding joy in the small moments is part of what it means to live lives of faithfulness and hope.

Prayer: Dear God, it is easy to get so wrapped up in everything we need to get done that we can forget to smile. We need to remember that you desire fullness of life for us, and one of the ways we experience that is through the gift of joy.

Help us to find your joy in the midst of our work: to see the beauty around us that reminds us of your presence in all things.

May we be signs of your joy to others with whom we work so that in us they may see your reflected Spirit. May we always point to the positive in our work environments, that others may be lifted up and refreshed by our presence.

It is easy, Lord, to get caught up in the negative aspects of our lives. We need your grace to refocus our vision. We also need your strength to bear our responsibilities cheerfully and with patience.

Give us the ability to stay tuned in to the present, that we may not lose sight of all the good things that come our way. We thank you so much for all the blessings you have given us, and we offer our prayer in the name of our friend and brother, Jesus. Amen.

Decision-Making
(For Discernment)

*The fruit of the Spirit is love, joy, peace, patience, kindness,
generosity, faithfulness, gentleness, and self-control.*

Galatians 5:22–23

Meditation: God's Spirit is always ready to help us: guiding us, teaching us, inviting us to grow. All we have to do is ask for God's wisdom to light our paths, to show us how best to serve God and one another. Praying for God's grace to show us which way to proceed helps to ensure that we are working together to build up God's kingdom and not our own egos. God delights in the opportunity to take our hands and lead us in Spirit and in truth.

Prayer: Loving God, we come before you today with humble and sincere hearts as together we ask for your grace to guide our decision-making. We know that all true wisdom comes from you, and we are grateful for your willingness to lead us.

Show us the direction you would have us take. Give us clarity of minds and of hearts so we can see your Spirit at work in our midst. Bring a sense of peace and quiet to each of us so we can listen to the still, small voice within ourselves that is you.

We thank you for the task with which you have entrusted us, and we ask that you bless our efforts to follow your call. Help us to stay true to the vision of those who have begun your good work, as together we move into a future that is unknown and uncertain.

Many are the voices and the options that compete for our attention, and limited is our time. Keep us focused as together we respond to your invitation to faithful love.

We ask this in Jesus' name. Amen.

Meal Prayer

God said, "See, I have given you every plant yielding seed
that is upon the face of all the earth, and every tree with seed
in its fruit; you shall have them for food."

Genesis 1:29

Meditation: Sharing a meal together is an enjoyable experience that connects us to those with whom we eat. When we eat together, we can review what has happened that day: the funny, significant, or interesting events that make up our lives. When we set aside time to eat with our family or our friends, we are saying to them that they are important to us and we value spending time with them.

Prayer: God of creation, as we share in the bounty of your gifts today, we ask that you bless the food we are about to eat together and that you bless the time we spend with one another.

May our gathering be a true communion and an opportunity to nourish our spirits as well as our bodies, as we look to find you in our companions and in ourselves.

We give thanks for all those who had a hand in bringing this meal to our table today: for the farmers who grew the food and for the cooks who prepared it.

We pray that we may be ever mindful of those who do not have enough to eat, and that just as you have blessed us with your generosity, we will seek to bless those less fortunate with ours.

May we leave this table encouraged and enriched as we go forth to do your work. May the energy we derive from this food sustain us in our ministries.

Grow in us the awareness that you are the giver of all that is good and foster in us a sense of gratitude for the many ways you have gifted us. We thank you and we bless you. Amen.

When Problems Arise

God is our refuge and strength,
a very present help in trouble.

Psalm 46:1

Meditation: How do we as a department, group, or organization handle problems? Do we face them head on, asking for God's help along the way, or do we ignore them, hoping they will go away? It is when we grapple together with our difficulties that we are able to grow and learn. Relying on God's grace and guidance to communicate honestly and openly with one another can go a long way toward solving many of the problems that we encounter.

Prayer: We come together in your name, Lord God, to ask for your help during this difficult time. You are a God of clarity and truth, and we pray that you will light our way today.

Even when things seem muddled, you are ever present, Lord; even when the future is cloudy and uncertain, you are always available to offer guidance.

Embrace and enfold each one of us in a blanket of your peace and understanding, that we may come together as a community to face our challenges. Send your Spirit of love and strength to us this day as we look to you for help.

May our concern and care for one another be the motivating force that leads to solutions that are for the good of all. Help us to look past our differences because we know that it is you whom we serve, you whom we seek.

We pray that your grace may enable us to see the bigger picture and enable us to do the work you have called us to do, which is carrying on the mission of Jesus at this time and in this place.

We thank you, as always, for the opportunity to do your work. Inspire us with your vision so we may always see the bigger picture.

We ask this in Jesus' name. Amen.

That We May Be One

I...beg you to lead a life worthy of the calling to which you have been called...making every effort to maintain the unity of the Spirit in the bond of peace.

Ephesians 4:1, 3

Meditation: What helps make a good team? What are the ingredients that promote unity within our organization? Each of us offers a unique perspective on the work we do, and we all bring different talents, skills, and vision to our jobs and to our group.

In Jesus' prayer for his disciples, he asked "that they may become completely one" (John 17:23) so that they may fulfill the mission to which they have been called. Individually and collectively, we need to continue to ask for God's grace that enables us to come together in mutual respect and openness.

Prayer: Loving God, you are ever present in our midst, walking with us, guiding us, affirming us. We pray that we may be ever mindful of your love that calls us forth to a new way of being and doing, a way that seeks unity and not division, and that you will always inspire us to actions that foster our common good.

In our ministry to others and each other, show us your vision of what we are to be about so we may stay focused on the building of your kingdom. Inspire us to always seek to resolve that which divides us, that together we can function in freedom and in truth.

If reconciliation is called for, help us to forgive one another, knowing that together we are more than we are alone. Let us see past our differences with laughter and with humility, knowing we do not hold all the answers within ourselves.

May we always look to you, the God of love and of light, to lead us together, so that we may witness your goodness to the world. Amen.

The Good, Green Earth

Thus says the LORD: Heaven is my throne, and the earth is my footstool....All these things my hand has made, and so all these things are mine, says the LORD.

Isaiah 66:1, 2

Meditation: How fortunate we are that God has created such a beautiful world in which we live! We are gifted with so many wonders of creation: seas and lakes, mountains, forests, plains, and canyons. Even in the most crowded cities, signs of God's life are evident in the trees and the flowers, the birds, and the squirrels. All of us need to appreciate and treasure the gifts we have been given in this glorious earth, and we need to work together to learn how to sustain these gifts.

Prayer: God our Creator, we have inherited a world of great beauty and splendor for which we are so grateful. It is you who are the author of the many natural wonders of our world—magnificent mountains, vast seas, rolling green pastures. We praise and thank you for your generosity in giving us this glorious planet on which we live.

Our greed and our need to consume have done untold damage to your earth: So much of our water is polluted, many species of your animals are extinct or endangered, and countless people are starving because others have plundered the resources they need to sustain themselves. We ask your forgiveness and the grace to learn from our mistakes.

Help us to be ever mindful, dear Lord, of the goodness of your creation, and foster in us the desire to uphold the beauty of this world we live in. Make us good stewards of all you have given us so we do not destroy this good green earth, but help us to treasure and maintain your global gifts so we can pass them on to future generations.

We pray these things through Christ, our Lord. Amen.

For Honesty, Integrity, and Faithful Witness

When Jesus saw the crowds, he went up the mountain;
and after he sat down, his disciples came to him.
Then he began to speak, and taught them, saying:
"Blessed are the pure in heart, for they will see God."

Matthew 5:1–2, 8

Meditation: So much of our contemporary society lives by the rule of putting ourselves first, without thinking about how our actions affect others. We are lost and moorless, for we have no foundation upon which to live our lives, no moral compass to uphold. We are "like sheep without a shepherd" (Matthew 9:36), just as the crowd was to whom Jesus preached. We need to base our lives and our actions on Gospel values, on loving others as we are loved, and learning how to be of service. Only then will we know true contentment and joy, for what we give to others, we give to ourselves.

Prayer: Lord of wisdom, teach us to walk in your ways so that our actions may always glorify you. May we desire to witness to others your love so that they may draw closer to you. Take from us whatever hinders us from adhering to your word. Create in us the desire to serve others and, in doing so, serving you.

Our world desperately needs models of truth and integrity, people of honor whose lives attest to your goodness. May we always seek to be persons who inspire others to faithful obedience of that which Jesus taught us.

Help us follow those who have begun this good work, those men and women who, before us, were determined to advance Jesus' mission of healing, teaching, or caring for the poor. Guide us to be your light so that we may witness to others your truth and your life.

We pray this through Jesus Christ, our Lord. Amen.

A Celebration of Diversity

Indeed, the body does not consist of one member but of many....
As it is, there are many members, yet one body....Now you are
the body of Christ and individually members of it.

1 Corinthians 12:14, 20, 27

Meditation: Our willingness to accept others who are different from us says a lot about our ability to accept ourselves. When we are able to embrace our coworkers' differences of opinion, personality, gender, race, or religion, we grow together in charity and in peace. All of God's daughters and sons are wonderful creations of God's goodness and wisdom, and God invites us to look past what is obvious to the truth of who a person is. Each of us longs for affirmation and acceptance, and we are called to extend these same gifts to all those we encounter each day.

Prayer: God, whose sun rises and sets upon us all, grant us the grace to see the giftedness of every single person you have created in this wide and wonderful world. Help us not to fear those who are dissimilar from ourselves, but give us the wisdom to see each person as a marvelous example of your handiwork.

Each of your children, Lord, is a unique part of the mosaic of your imagination, and we are grateful for the vastness of your dreams reflected in us. Teach us generosity of spirit so we can embrace the myriad of giftedness in all human beings.

Humbly we are mindful that, because we do not contain all of life's answers within ourselves, we need one another to grow and to learn. Open our minds and our hearts to all those we meet, so that we can discover the bounty of your presence in each person, and our joy will be increased.

We ask this in the name of our brother and our Savior, Jesus. Amen.

God's Call to Use Our Gifts

You are the light of the world. A city built on a hill cannot be hid.
No one after lighting a lamp puts it under the bushel basket, but
on the lampstand, and it gives light to all in the house. In the
same way, let your light shine before others, so that they may see
your good works and give glory to your Father in heaven.

Matthew 5:14–16

Meditation: Each of us has been chosen to fulfill our portion of God's plans of goodness for humanity, and God has given each of us the gifts we need to complete our task. Yet sometimes we shy away from using our talents for the good of all. We need God's grace so we may have the courage to let our light shine, the light God has bestowed upon us to do our job here on earth.

Prayer: Spirit of the risen Christ, help us to discern the ways we are called to carry out your mission of love. Clarify for us how you intend for us to follow in your footsteps, so that we may know when we are headed in the right direction.

Strengthen in us the resolve to answer your invitation to use our gifts every moment of every day. Some days we might be tired, and it may be harder for us to shoulder the burdens that accompany our work. Walk with us always as we look to you for guidance in how best to reflect your vision of goodness for our lives.

May we desire to give of ourselves in ways that show your presence in us to the world. May we know that your love is all that we need to do the work you have called each of us to do.

We pray all these things in the name of your Son, Jesus. Amen.

Listening to the Spirit Within

Likewise the Spirit helps us in our weakness; for we do not know how to pray as we ought, but that very Spirit intercedes with sighs too deep for words. And God, who searches the heart, knows what is the mind of the Spirit, because the Spirit intercedes for the saints according to the will of God.

Romans 8:26–27

Meditation: If we are to stay true to the mission with which Jesus has called us, every day we must be mindful of the still, small voice within us who is God. Many voices, many agendas compete for our attention, but collectively and consistently we must quiet ourselves to hear the Voice of truth who longs to guide us on our way.

Prayer: Spirit of truth and life, we thank you for your presence within us that challenges us, loves us and leads us together in service to your people. We ask that we may always have the wisdom to take the time to truly listen to you, for ours is a world hungering for your goodness and your healing.

May we be mindful that as instruments of your love here on earth, we bear a responsibility to seek your guidance in all our ministries. Strengthen within each of us the desire to follow you and show us how we can best accomplish this work you have begun.

Help us to learn to pay attention to the many ways you show yourself to us, for we know that you are with us always. Let us be encouraged by your presence as we care for those whom you have entrusted to us.

Holy Spirit, we marvel at the ways you have called us to bring your light to the world. Teach us to listen to your presence within so we may witness to your love.

We ask this in the name of Jesus, who is with us now and forever. Amen.

Going the Extra Mile

Therefore, since we are surrounded by so great a cloud of witnesses, let us...run with perseverance the race that is set before us, looking to Jesus the pioneer and perfecter of our faith.

Hebrews 12:1–2

Meditation: Together we are called to a mighty purpose, a wonderful endeavor: ministering, in love, to the people of God with whom we work. Every person we meet is uniquely created and of infinite value, and each is worthy of our respect and deserves to be treated with dignity. God has given us the opportunity to make a difference in others' lives as we strive to further God's mission in our workplace.

Prayer: God of mercy and compassion, we cannot begin to fathom the tenderness and love you have for each one of us. We have been given a glimpse of our true worth in the person of Jesus, your Son who walked this earth so many years ago and whose Spirit is with us still.

Inspire in us the desire to give as Jesus did, completely and unreservedly, so that together we may love thoroughly, heal compassionately, and instruct wisely. Make each of us the bearer of your Good News to a world longing for wholeness and peace.

Give us your strength on those days when our energy is flagging, and remind us that it is your work, not ours, that we do. We know not the end results of our attempts to minister in your name, yet we believe that your love and your presence are enough to see us through.

Set individuals on our path who will model for us what it means to serve your people, and help us to likewise encourage those who seek to be your light to others.

All of this we ask in the name of your Son, Jesus, our Lord. Amen.

The Gift of New Vision

*For now we see in a mirror, dimly, but then we will see
face to face. Now I know only in part; then I will know fully,
even as I have been fully known.*

1 Corinthians 13:12

Meditation: All of us, at one time or another, need the gift of new vision, for there are times that each of us lacks the ability to see our own or others' true beauty. Jesus longs to take the scales from our eyes that can imprison us in our darkness, that keep us from enjoying the brilliance of the world and of the people around us. When we see clearly, we are more able to act rightly.

Prayer: We come to you, God, with open hearts and outstretched arms, for we need your vision in our lives. It is only your grace that allows us to see as you would have us see. It is your sight, given to us, that makes us aware of the blessings you have bestowed on us, and opens our eyes to the needs of others with whom we come in contact.

Let us not see as the world sees, for too often it is oblivious to others' material or spiritual poverty. Along with our eyes, transform our hearts: stretch them, soften them, that we may be responsive to the urgent cries of those who suffer in our midst.

We thank you for your willingness to change our perception of all we see, so that joyfully we can claim the freedom that is our rightful inheritance. Catch us when we stumble and fall due to our blindness, and lead us forward to truth and new life. Help us to trust that the light of your Spirit will illuminate our path, so that together we may walk with purpose and conviction.

All this we pray in the name of your Son, Jesus. Amen.

Taking Risks

Do not, therefore, abandon that confidence of yours;
it brings a great reward. For you need endurance,
so that when you have done the will of God,
you may receive what was promised.

Hebrews 10:35–36

Meditation: Where did the misconception come from that Christians are bashful and demure? After all, on the day of Pentecost Jesus' Spirit came to his apostles "like the rush of a violent wind" (Acts 2:2). Sometimes we are called to courageous acts of boldness as we seek to further God's kingdom on earth, knowing that God is with us every step of our journey, enlivening and emboldening us to face the tasks at hand.

Prayer: God whose strength animates and inspires us, be with us in this new venture we have undertaken for the sake of your people. We know not what the future holds, only that you will be there with us, leading, guiding, and challenging us.

Together we have discerned that you have called us to this enterprise so we can better serve the ones you cherish, and we thank you for this opportunity to witness to your love. We ask that your grace permeate our endeavors so that all we do will be in the name of love.

At times we will stumble as we journey together on this new adventure, but we ask that you catch us with swiftness and sureness before we fall. May we always look to you for direction with each new twist and turn we take, knowing you will lead us and light our way.

Give us the courage to face whatever challenges lie ahead, and imbue in us the determination to persevere as together we accomplish this work to which you have summoned us.

We ask these things with hopeful sincerity, and we pray in the name of your Son, Jesus. Amen.

Picking Ourselves Up and Dusting Ourselves Off

You have been born anew, not of perishable
but of imperishable seed, through the living and
enduring word of God.

1 Peter 1:23

Meditation: Sometimes in the course of completing a project, we may realize that what we had in mind when we started is not at all what we produced. Or we may work long and hard on a proposal, only to find it is not well-received or recognized. It is hard not to let our individual egos become bruised when our efforts are not universally applauded. We must always remember that our contributions are not about us but about following the call of Jesus to further his mission.

Prayer: Good and gracious God, we long to be co-creators with you in your plans of goodness for humanity, but we do not always see as you see as our vision is limited. Help us to forgive ourselves and each other when all does not go as planned. Restore in us the seeds of hope so that we may do good in our limited time here on earth.

We know we may stumble and fall as we seek to build your kingdom, yet keep our hearts forever focused on your love and care for us as we attempt to do your work. Help us to always cherish ourselves and each other, for we are made in your image and likeness. Do not let us to fall prey to the blame game that locks us into resentment and surliness, for to do so stifles our growth and blocks our progress.

It is only with you by our side that we are able to accomplish anything worthwhile, for it is your strength that allows us to follow your dreams of fullness for your people. Bless us, though we are limited and imperfect, as we go about your business of loving and helping others.

We ask this in Jesus' name. Amen.

To Help Us See the Bigger Picture

Because we look not at what can be seen
but at what cannot be seen;
for what can be seen is temporary,
but what cannot be seen is eternal.

2 Corinthians 4:18

Meditation: God has a glorious plan for all of us that we cannot begin to fathom. Our participation in God's intentions for humanity is part of a mystery that continues to unfold, the whole of which we do not fully understand. Much of our response to God's call to love others as we have been loved is made in faith: faith that we are doing the right thing, faith that our work is meaningful, and faith that allows us to get up every morning to face a new day.

Prayer: God of Abraham and Sarah, of Lazarus, Mary, and Martha, we praise you for your bountiful wisdom and for your loving kindness to all whom you have created. We trust that you have only goodness in mind for each and every one of us. Help us not to become bogged down in the tiny details of our lives, but to always keep in mind that there is a larger purpose to which you have called us.

Though each of us is a small part of the universal whole, help us to remember that we are "fearfully and wonderfully made" (Psalm 139:14), and that you rely on all of us to bring forth your vision of goodness.

Expand our vision of the purpose of our responsibilities so that we may engage in them with joy and perseverance. Enliven our minds and our wills as we go about our work, and give us the grace to trust that your hand is upon us.

Give us the patience to encourage others in their daily tasks, and may we always look to you for sustenance as we live out our vocation of service to others.

We ask all this in Jesus' name. Amen.

Who Are My Brothers and My Sisters?

For I was hungry and you gave me food,
I was thirsty and you gave me something to drink,
I was a stranger and you welcomed me,
I was naked and you gave me clothing,
I was sick and you took care of me,
I was in prison and you visited me.

Matthew 25:35–36

Meditation: We do not have to travel far to encounter others in need, though there are people all over the world who suffer and could use our support. Our next-door neighbor could be imprisoned by her loneliness, our coworker down the hall could be hungry for a smile. Attending to the hungry, the thirsty, the stranger, the naked, the sick, and the prisoner among us is a matter of opening our hearts and, perhaps, stepping outside of our comfort zones as we remember that Christ comes to us in many forms.

Prayer: Jesus, whose love enfolds and embraces us all, open our minds and our hearts to the people who struggle right here in our midst. Whether it is our complacency or our lethargy that blinds us to the needs of others, make us sensitive to those who suffer in any way, as we remember that "there but for the grace of God go I."

Mindful of your compassion for us in our human weaknesses, give us the gift of compassion for all who lack the basic resources of food, water, and shelter. Giver of life and source of all goodness, show us the way to freedom that longs for hope and sustenance for all humankind.

May our efforts to assist those in need attract like-minded individuals so that, together, we may help more than we could alone. Bless us with the necessary resources so that by your aid, we may be able to bless others with the loving care they deserve.

We ask these things in the name of Jesus. Amen.

During Times of Transition

So we can say with confidence, "The Lord is my helper;
I will not be afraid. What can anyone do to me?"
Jesus Christ is the same yesterday and today and forever.

Hebrews 13:6, 8

Meditation: Most of us, if we are honest with ourselves, do not like change. We prefer stability and the comfort of what is known to times of change and uncertainty. We may even feel resentful if change is thrust upon us without our consent. Even in the midst of unrest and turmoil, we can count on the constancy of Jesus, for he has promised to be with us until the end of time. Though we may be daunted at the winds around us as Peter was when Jesus beckoned him to walk on water, like Peter, we are steadied by Jesus when we call out to him.

Prayer: God of everlasting faithfulness, you have called us to new ways of being and doing to which we are still becoming acclimated. We know that you are with us in the midst of this transition and we thank you for your presence.

Guide us as we journey together upon this sea of change, for we need your wisdom and your steadfast love as we move forward toward an unknown future. Give us the courage to face our challenges with grace, and help us to trust that your hand is always upon us.

May we look to you for reassurance so that we may encourage any among us who falter in this time of uncertainty, and strengthen our conviction that with you by our side, we have nothing to fear. Encourage us to come together as a team as we remember that it is your people whom we serve.

All this we ask in the name of your Son, Jesus, our Lord. Amen.

Random Acts of Kindness

But those who do what is true come to the light, so that it may be clearly seen that their deeds have been done in God.

John 3:21

Meditation: All of us know how it brightens our day when someone shows us an unexpected kindness. Others' kind actions for us can be small like someone holding the door open or a coworker sharing a treat with us. Since we know the value of people being kind to us, we recognize how important it is that we be kind to others, even in small, almost unrecognizable ways.

Prayer: Lord of kindness and compassion, transform our hearts so that we may always seek to treat others as we would like to be treated. Help us to think before we speak, so that our words may be clothed in kindness to one another. Be the light that beckons us to actions of goodness to everyone we meet, so we may bring gladness and lift others' burdens in ways we may never know.

Enlarge our spirits and broaden our vision so that we may spread joy in surprising ways, as the possibilities for kindness are as infinite as the grains of sand on a beach. Teach us that as we practice kindness, we increase our happiness, and we make a difference in the world.

When we compliment a stranger, do someone else's chore, or shovel a neighbor's snow, we not only show your goodness, Lord, we build others' trust in the goodness of humanity. Show us that our kindness has a domino effect that is unending, and that even simple acts of thoughtfulness change people's lives.

May we always seek our inspiration from you, Creator of all that is kind and good, as we try to teach others the ways of kindness.

We ask this in the name of your Son, Jesus, our Lord. Amen.

Give Us Patience, Lord!

Bear one another's burdens, and in this way
you will fulfill the law of Christ.

Galatians 6:2

Meditation: Some days it is a challenge to be patient with one another. We might be tired, or we might consider another person's behavior less than considerate. Other days we might feel impatient with the organization for whom we work (*what, another meeting?*). The gift of patience can feel like an elusive prize just beyond our reach. As God is patient with us, we need to ask God for the grace to "bear one another's burdens" so we can be patient with each other.

Prayer: God of patience and love, soften our hearts and heal all within us that tends to find fault with one another. Help us to cultivate an attitude of patience with ourselves, so that we will be able to be patient with each other.

Daily we face many challenges and frustrations, and we may be tempted to lash out in irritation when it all feels like too much to handle. When this happens, give us the ability to stop, breathe, and ask you for help, knowing that you, the God of peace, will grant us patience when we need it.

Gift us with a sense of humor that looks past others' foibles, and help us to carry our burdens lightly. Enable us to see others' giftedness and not their faults, and bestow in us grateful hearts that allow us to appreciate those with whom we work.

May we get the rest we need when our bodies are weary, and may you refresh our spirits when they need renewal. Most of all, help us to recognize that with your strength, we can cope with anything that comes our way.

This we pray in the name of your Son, Jesus. Amen.

Commitment to Our Mission

After this the Lord appointed seventy others and sent them on
ahead of him in pairs to every town and place where he himself
intended to go. He said to them, "The harvest is plentiful, but
the laborers are few; therefore ask the Lord of the harvest to send
out laborers into his harvest. Go on your way."

Luke 10:1–3

Meditation: Jesus calls us to go where "he himself intended to go," meaning we continue the ministry of Jesus in our service to others. Many are the problems we will encounter along our journey, but the Lord promises to be with us always. When we work together to further Jesus' mission, we are able to accomplish so much more than when we work alone: That is why Jesus appointed the seventy to travel in pairs.

Prayer: Spirit of the risen Christ, we look to you now and always for hope and courage as we dedicate ourselves to the mission to which you have entrusted us. Inspire us with zeal to make a difference in the lives of those whom we touch. Enkindle our hearts with the fire of your love, that we may always have the enthusiasm to serve others in your name.

May our contact with others further our own transformation to become more and more the persons you have called us to be, and in our care of your people may we be witnesses to your compassion.

Steady our course when we stumble and make smooth our path when we fall. Help us to keep our eyes fixed upon you and you alone as we strive to minister in your name. Give us the grace to encourage one another when our energy flags, knowing that our purpose is divinely inspired.

We thank you for the invitation to do your work, and we ask that we may always seek to be worthy of the gift of your call to us.

All of this we pray in the name of Jesus, our mentor and our leader. Amen.

May We Stay Positive

I will give thanks to the LORD with my whole heart; I will tell
of all your wonderful deeds. I will be glad and exult in you;
I will sing praise to our name, O Most High.

Psalm 9:1–2

Meditation: A positive attitude is contagious, but so is a negative one. Our attitude is a choice we make day after day, hour after hour, minute by minute. Are we able to think before we speak so that the words we choose serve to lift others up and not bring them down? Do we recognize what a powerful influence our outlook has on our emotional, spiritual, and physical well-being? As Christians, we are called to be joyful witnesses to the world, since we know that by Jesus' resurrection, there is no room in our lives for gloom and despair.

Prayer: Spirit of the living God, we thank you for our lives and for the opportunity to serve you through our ministry to others. Together we ask that you gift us with enthusiasm for the many tasks we have at hand.

Refresh our minds, bodies, and spirits when they need rest so that we are not tempted to allow fatigue to speak louder than our love. Give us the ability to stay focused on what we are about: ministering as instruments of your purpose to those who need your care.

Imbue us with your joy so we may bring cheerfulness to all we meet, and may our gladness especially touch the hearts of those whose spirits need lifting up this day.

Help us recognize that you are always with us, ready and available to answer our needs when we call upon you for support, so we may be witness of your resurrected Spirit in our midst.

All of this we pray in the name of the risen Christ. Amen.

Prayers for God's People

For Expectant Parents

When a woman is in labor, she has pain, because her hour has come. But when her child is born, she no longer remembers the anguish because of the joy of having brought a human being into the world.

John 16:21

Meditation: Jesus held children in high regard: he told his disciples in Matthew 18 that we need to become like children to enter the kingdom of God. Those of us who are expecting children can remember his words as we joyfully anticipate the birth of our child.

Prayer: Loving God, we come before you today to ask your blessing on us as we prepare for our child to be born. We ask for the gift of good health and that you will bless this child mightily with your love.

Help us to instruct our child in your ways, God, and give us the wisdom to rear our child well. We are humbly grateful that you have chosen us to be parents of this child, and we do not take our responsibility lightly.

Give us patience and strength for the sleepless nights that lie ahead and the many tasks that await us in caring for our child. Help us to learn from others who have already walked the path of parenthood so we may benefit from their experience.

May our child know that he or she is loved beyond all telling, and may we teach our child about your love as well. We pray that our child will grow into a happy, fulfilled adult, and we thank you for our role in making sure that happens.

We ask that our child will be blessed with friends, Lord, and know all the joys and innocence of childhood. We also ask that we open ourselves to what our child has to teach us about life so we may grow as individuals.

We pray all these things in Jesus' name. Amen.

For Children/Youth

Jesus said, "Let the little children come to me, and do not stop them; for it is to such as these that the kingdom of heaven belongs."

Matthew 19:14

Meditation: Our children are our most precious natural resource and a tremendous gift from God. Few things can bring us more joy than a smile or laughter from a child. Yet sadly, many children and youth around the world are neglected and abused, and many more live in poverty with not enough to eat. We must never forget our obligation to care for the least of these, our children and youth.

Prayer: Loving God, we thank you for the gift of our children, and we ask that we may always treasure how special and important they are.

Those of who parent know that as we form our children, they are forming us. We thank you, Lord, for using our children to teach us about life and love.

May each child you have created recognize how precious he or she is in your eyes, and may all children everywhere feel loved and cherished. We ask you to especially bless those children who suffer, and we pray that we may be instruments of your goodness to all our young who need help in any way.

We also ask your blessing on all those who work with children: for teachers, health-care professionals, counselors, and social workers, for there are few greater responsibilities than the care of children.

Give our children and youth the perseverance and patience they need in school, and inspire them with enthusiasm for learning. Help us adults likewise to be inspired by our children and their eagerness, innocence, and joy.

We ask these things in the name of Jesus, your Son, who once was a child, too! Amen.

For Teens/Young Adults

*Let no one despise your youth, but set the believers an example
in speech and conduct, in love, in faith, in purity.*

1 Timothy 4:12

Meditation: Who has not been inspired by the joy, enthusiasm, and energy of our teens and young adults? They are truly a gift to us, and those of us who work with them are indeed privileged. We must always remember that with our young adults lies the future of the world, and all who are charged with their formation bear a special responsibility.

Prayer: Loving God, you inspire our teens and young adults with bold visions of the future. Help them to dream of possibilities yet unseen, and help us to always encourage them, so they will develop into the fullest version of who you have called them to be.

Let us never quash their enthusiasm and passion, but rather nurture their hopes for what may lie ahead. We pray that we may be good role models for our teens and young adults, knowing they still look to us for guidance and direction.

Likewise, we ask for the grace to be open to what our teens and young adults have to teach us about life and about ourselves. May we never take our young women and men for granted, but always treat them with the respect and dignity they deserve.

We also pray for the world our young adults will inherit, and that those of us who are older will strive to make our corner of it better than when we first arrived. We ask that our teens will receive the courage and wisdom they need to grapple with the world's problems they will encounter.

Most importantly, help us to nurture our teens' and young adults' thirst for intimacy with you, O God, for their faith will be their stronghold for the future.

We pray these things through Christ, our Lord. Amen.

For the Elderly

So even to old age and gray hairs, O God, do not forsake me,
until I proclaim your might to all the generations to come.

Psalm 71:18

Meditation: Many people enjoy a vital old age, well-loved by family and friends, but unfortunately many others do not. Poor health, loneliness, and financial concerns can all cloud the horizon for elderly people. Our God is a faithful, compassionate God who longs to be very present to us as we age, and who journeys with us in the midst of whatever physical or emotional challenges we may face as we get older.

Prayer: We thank you, Lord, for the many gifts our elderly bring to us: their experience, wisdom, and knowledge. We treasure their stories of a bygone era when the world was a different place than it is now.

Help us to always value the contributions of our older generation, as they have much to teach us. May we treat our elderly with the respect and dignity they deserve and that, sadly, they don't always receive.

Give us the grace we need to treat ourselves, as we age, with gentle patience. Bless our efforts to reach out to the elderly who struggle with depression and with physical limitations, knowing that some day we may very well walk in their shoes.

We are grateful for the wonderful relationships we enjoy with our elders, those between grandchildren and grandparents and between parents and children. The love we share with our aged relatives is a sign of your presence, grace, and love in our midst.

As a country, we pray for the resources we need to take good care of our older folks so they will never be neglected or abused, but cherished and honored as they deserve.

We pray these things through Christ, our Lord. Amen.

For Those Who Grieve

Blessed be the God and Father of our Lord Jesus Christ,
the Father of mercies and the God of all consolation,
who consoles us in all our affliction, so that we may be able
to console those who are in any affliction with the consolation
with which we ourselves are consoled by God.

2 Corinthians 1:3–4

Meditation: When we are grieving a loss, we may feel very alone in our sadness, but we need to know that God is always with us to comfort and console us. Rather than withdrawing from others and from God, we need to reach out for support and allow God, our friends and family to help us. In this way we will know that our grief won't last forever.

Prayer: God of compassion, be with us as we mourn our loss, for our hearts are torn apart and we need your strength. Walk with us in our healing journey so that we will know we are not alone in our sorrow.

We ask that the memories of the one we have lost live on in our hearts so we will feel our loved one's presence always. We know our loved one is with you, loving God, and we thank you for welcoming your servant into your kingdom.

Help us to know, Lord, that our sadness will gradually lift, and may hope and joy be with us again one day. In the midst of our poverty of spirit, we pray that we may know your grace and blessings so that we may endure.

May our hearts be softened in our grief, Lord, so that someday we will be able to show your compassion to others who mourn. Help us to see your face in all who long to help us through our bereavement.

We pray these things through Christ, our Lord. Amen.

For the Lonely

Do not fear, for I am with you, do not be afraid,
for I am your God; I will strengthen you, I will help you,
I will uphold you with my victorious right hand.

Isaiah 41:10

Meditation: Everyone experiences occasional feelings of loneliness, but for some people it is a chronically painful state of being. We human beings were made to be in relationship, but geographical distance, financial hurdles, family tensions and conflicts all contribute to perpetual feelings of isolation and loneliness for so many. Our God is a compassionate and faithful God who longs to comfort us in the midst of whatever loneliness we may feel.

Prayer: Sometimes, God, the loving voice of those we care about or even a stranger's smile can seem very far away. At those difficult times, we may feel distanced from you as well. Teach us to know we can always count on you to be with us whenever we are lonely.

Help us recognize others' loneliness, so we can reach out with a smile, a gesture, or a sign of our caring, for no one is exempt from loneliness from time to time. Teach us also to offer the gift of hospitality to neighbors, coworkers, students, parishioners, or anyone who is new in a given situation, so they will feel welcomed and not alone.

As Jesus underwent the ultimate experience of loneliness in his death on the cross, he understands what it is like to feel abandoned and alone, and he is there to help us in our time of need. Give us the grace to trust in Jesus' words, "Remember, I am with you always, to the end of the age" (Matthew 28:20).

Make of us instruments of your care and concern, Lord, especially to the shut-ins and to those with no family and no friends.

All this we pray in the name of your loving Son, Jesus, our Lord. Amen.

For the Sick

Even though I walk through the darkest valley, I fear no evil;
for you are with me; your rod and your staff—they comfort me.

Psalm 23:4

Meditation: Few things make us feel more vulnerable than being sick. Those of us who work with the sick have a special calling—to be instruments of God's healing. Nurses, doctors, physical, speech, and occupational therapists, social workers, and chaplains all participate in continuing Jesus' mission to help the sick and suffering of our world.

Prayer: Loving God, we believe that you desire only wholeness and goodness for us, and so we lift up to you all who are ill in any way. Grant them comfort and strength in their affliction, O God, and please restore them to good health.

We also ask that you bless all those who work with the sick, that they will be strengthened in their ministry. Help them know how vitally important their challenging roles are as they seek to be signs of your compassion in the world.

Help those who are sick to trust in you, God, as they journey toward recovery. Grant peace to the families of those who are ill, Lord, as they wait in hope for their loved one's healing.

Loving God, we ask your very special blessing on those who are dying and are soon to see you face to face. Give them peace, Lord, and surround them with the knowledge of your presence and love.

We also pray for our health-care system, that it may always function for the good of those who are sick. We lift up to you those who cannot afford health insurance or proper medical care, and ask that we may be especially mindful of their needs.

We pray these things in the name of your Son, our Lord. Amen.

For Health-care Workers

Honor physicians for their services, for the Lord created them;
for their gift of healing comes from the Most High.

Sirach 38:1–2

Meditation: Not only physicians but all health-care workers have a most sacred duty, that of caring for the sick and suffering. First Corinthians tells us that the gift of healing comes from God (1 Corinthians 12:2), and so all who participate in the ministry of healing are doing God's work.

Yet health-care workers face many challenges in today's world: stressful jobs, an aging patient population, the problems of many who are uninsured, and a rise in substance abuse to name just a few. Medical personnel need to know that God is with them and that they are participating in the healing ministry of Jesus.

Prayer: Loving God, we ask a special blessing on all who care for the sick, and we pray that you will help them to know how important their work is.

Inspire nurses, doctors, therapists, social workers, chaplains, and everyone who helps to bring about healing. Please guide the hands and hearts of all health-care professionals so they will remember they are doing God's work.

Help our nation and our world address the problems in health care today: its rising costs and lack of access to medical care for so many. We pray for women and men of courage and creativity who will work to bring about health-care reform so that treatment is available to all and not just a few.

Bestow the gift of compassion on all who share in the healing mission of Jesus so that those who are sick may always be treated with dignity and respect. Ease the burdens of those medical professionals who risk burning out because of their demanding jobs, and help them remember to care for themselves as they care for others.

We pray these things in the loving name of your Son, Jesus. Amen.

For Teachers

I want their hearts to be encouraged and united in love,
so that they may have all the riches of assured understanding
and have the knowledge of God's mystery, that is, Christ himself,
in whom are hidden all the treasures of wisdom and knowledge.

Colossians 2:2–3

Meditation: After parents, teachers probably have the most profound influence on the formation of young people. The calling of teachers is sacred and their responsibility is great. Those who can look back fondly upon the wise instruction of a beloved teacher are lucky indeed. Our teachers need encouragement and affirmation, for theirs can be a difficult job without much recognition. We are thankful for teachers and for the important gifts they bring to their ministry.

Prayer: Loving God, all wisdom and knowledge comes from you, to be imparted to those who instruct our young. Bless all teachers, so that as they guide those for whom they are responsible, they also will be guided by your grace.

Help our teachers to always see your face, Jesus, in the faces of those they teach. May all teachers understand that they instruct others much more by who they are than by what they say.

Strengthen all educators with enthusiasm for their ministry, and hold them up on the days they need encouragement and sustenance. Give them patience when managing their classrooms and perseverance when grading their papers.

May teachers know the support of school administrators and parents alike, so there will be true collaboration between all those involved in the formation of young people. We also pray for adequate resources that will enable all instructors to do their jobs well.

Most importantly, God, let your love be the guiding principle that informs and upholds the ministry of teachers.

We pray these things in the name of Jesus, our Savior and our Teacher. Amen.

For Office Workers

*Whoever speaks must do so as one speaking the very words of God;
whoever serves must do so with the strength that God supplies,
so that God may be glorified in all things through Jesus Christ.*

1 Peter 4:11

Meditation: Oftentimes, it is our office workers—administrative assistants, secretaries, receptionists, and clerks who make up the backbone of any organization. Many times they are the unsung heroes in our institutions and the ones who keep things running smoothly so that the system as a whole functions properly. We thank them for their dedication and behind-the-scenes leadership skills, as we know that our office workers' contributions are absolutely essential to the success of our organizations.

Prayer: Each of us has been called by God to use our particular talents and skills in various ways to further the mission of Jesus. We are particularly grateful for the gifts our office workers bring to our schools, hospitals, and churches, and we know that without them these institutions could not survive.

Bless our secretaries and administrative assistants with the knowledge that their efforts are sorely needed and greatly appreciated. Give them patience for the times when things don't go well and grace to rise to the many challenges they face.

Help each of us to recognize that we are all part of the body of Christ, and as members of Christ's body we need each other so that we can each fulfill our various roles and responsibilities.

May cheerfulness be the guiding principle in all offices everywhere so that our hearts and the hearts of others may be lightened by our smiles and by our goodwill. In the midst of our close quarters, we ask for the grace to forgive one another our foibles and our failings.

All these things we pray in the loving name of your Son, Jesus. Amen.

For Artists, Writers, and Musicians

It is good to give thanks to the LORD, to sing praises to your name, O Most High....to the music of the lute and the harp, to the melody of the lyre. For you, O LORD, have made me glad by your work; at the works of your hands I sing for joy.

Psalm 92:1, 3–4

Meditation: All good gifts come from the Lord, and so it is with the creative gifts of art and music. Those who paint beautiful pictures or compose lovely songs enliven and enrich our lives immeasurably. We are grateful for the ways that artists, writers, and musicians are instruments of God's creative spirit at work.

Prayer: We praise and thank you, God, for the beauty and joy that art, music, and literature bring to us. We ask your special blessing on all those who express themselves through the creative arts.

Inspire artists, musicians and writers with your passion, Lord, and guide them with your wisdom, that their creations may truly reflect your beauty. We thank you, God, for how the arts contribute to our growth as humans, and also how they help us remember the soaring heights to which we can aspire.

In this world of increasing technology that can divide us at times, may the conceptions of people whose creative work is a manifestation of your spirit serve to animate and unite us. We pray that Jesus' saving mission can be enhanced and glorified through the expressions of our artists, writers, and musicians.

We are grateful for the healing power that the arts have for our bodies, minds, and spirits. We acknowledge the importance of beauty for contemplation, relaxation, and pure enjoyment.

Help us to encourage the architects of all things visual and auditory, that they will see how important their contributions are to all of us.

We pray these things in Jesus name. Amen.

For World Religions

*I ask not only on behalf of these, but also on behalf of those who
will believe in me through their word, that they may all be one.
As you, Father, are in me, and I am in you, may they also be in us.*

John 17:20–21

Meditation: We live in a world of great diversity and plurality of
thought, culture, and religion. We can be informed and enriched
by the multiplicity of beliefs and by the beauty found in different
faith traditions, or we can feel threatened and defensive that others'
ways are not our own. As we strive to respect divergent religious
paths, we contribute to peaceful coexistence with our brothers and
sisters all over the world.

Prayer: We humbly pray, Lord, that you will remove the scales
from our eyes that keep us focused on our differences with others rather than on our similarities so that we may learn wisdom
from one another.

Guide us to the truth that we are created in love, and that we
all seek intimacy with you in some fashion. Let gentleness guide
our ways, and let prudence inform our actions with our brothers
and sisters across the globe.

We thank you for people like Thich Nhat Hanh, the Dalai Lama,
Pope Francis, and other spiritual leaders all over the world, who
show us how to live and love. We pray that, as we open ourselves
to these holy people's guidance, we in turn may become more holy
ourselves.

When the Sadducees were arguing in his midst about various
religious teachings, Jesus admonished them to "love your neighbor
as yourself" (Mark 12:31), thus cutting to the core of their faith.
Help us to remember, Lord, that loving you and loving our neighbors are the most important things we can do.

We pray these things in the name of Jesus, your Son and our
Lord. Amen.

For Those Who Work the Land

God said, "See, I have given you every plant yielding seed that is upon the face of all the earth, and every tree with seed in its fruit; you shall have them for food."

Genesis 1:29

Meditation: We are indebted to farmers and all those involved in bringing food to our table. They keep our bodies nourished and fulfill an important role in caring for humanity. We are especially grateful to all those small farmers who struggle to stay afloat yet remain dedicated to their profession. We ask God's blessings for them today in a special way.

Prayer: Creator God, you have gifted humanity with every kind of vegetation under the sun, and we are grateful for your bounty. You have bestowed a special responsibility on all those who work the land and whose labors bring forth goodness we all enjoy.

Bless all those who have answered your call to keep humanity fed, and in the midst of their hard work, keep our farmers mindful that theirs is a *special* task that few can fulfill.

We especially pray for the many who have made personal sacrifices to keep their farms going, and we ask that they may receive the resources they need to survive. May our communities recognize the importance of supporting our local farmers so we can continue to reap the fruits of their labor.

Help us to be good stewards of this earth you have entrusted to us so that it will remain intact for all future generations. We thank you for those whose work is instrumental in sustaining and supporting the land, and we ask that you continue to show us ways to lovingly care for this wonderful world you have given us.

All this we pray in the holy name of your Son, Jesus. Amen.

For Animals/Creatures

God made the wild animals of the earth of every kind,
and the cattle of every kind, and everything that creeps upon
the ground of every kind. And God saw that it was good.

Genesis 1:25

Meditation: We are blessed to live alongside the birds and animals of this world. Many of us have pets or at least know the joy of animal companionship, whether it be a dog, cat, bird, rodent, or fish. Like all of God's gifts, we should never take for granted any living creature but treat each of them with dignity and respect.

Prayer: Creator God, you have gifted us with animals so that we may know more fully the wonders of this world. May we remember that we are called to revere these co-inhabitants of our earth.

We ask your special blessing on all species that are endangered, Lord, and we ask your forgiveness for those animals we have hunted to extinction. Give us the wisdom we need to care well for future generations of all your creatures.

For those of us who are pet owners, we thank you for the joys of our nonhuman friends. For those of us who raise cattle, pigs, sheep, or horses, may we always treat our animals with kindness.

Help us to learn from animals the lessons they have to teach us about life: the importance of affection, the need to act responsibly, how to live with others who are different from us. May we remember, like animals, how to play and how to live in the moment.

Thank you, Lord, for the gift of animals and for all they bring to us. As we grow in our concern for our world and all your living creatures, help us to learn to revere life in all forms.

We pray these things in the name of your Son, Jesus, our Lord. Amen.

Celebrating the Saints and Holy People

Mary, the Holy Mother of God

January 1

*And Mary said, "My soul magnifies the Lord, and
my spirit rejoices in God my Savior...Surely, from now on
all generations will call me blessed; for the Mighty One
has done great things for me."*

Luke 1:46–48, 49

Meditation: All of us have a purpose, a unique destiny that God has in mind for us. Each of us has been called to play an important role for the future of humanity.

We look to Mary, the Mother of Jesus, as a model of openness to God's call, as someone who said "yes" to God though she didn't know how her future would unfold or exactly what saying "yes" would entail. Mary is a witness to us of humble trust in the Lord as she helped to fulfill God's plan of salvation for the world.

Prayer: God who calls each of us to a future unforeseen and un-imagined, help us to respond positively when you invite us to new ventures for the sake of your people. We need your grace to say "yes" when you ask us to open ourselves, in love, to different ways of helping our brothers and sisters.

Give us the ability to rely on your strength and not our own when we feel daunted by the task of furthering your mission. Help us to trust, like Mary, that you will always be with us in the twists and turns of our lives of ministry.

Just as Mary glorified you by her response to your invitation to be the Mother of Jesus, may we glorify you as we work to build your kingdom here on earth. You are a compassionate, faithful God, and we are grateful that we are called to serve in your name.

All this we pray in the name of Mary's Son and our Lord, Jesus. Amen.

St. Elizabeth Ann Seton

January 4

The Lord is my shepherd, I shall not want. Even though I walk through the darkest valley, I fear no evil; for you are with me; your rod and your staff—they comfort me.

Psalm 23:1, 4

Meditation: The first American-born person to be canonized a saint, Elizabeth Ann Seton's favorite Scripture passage was Psalm 23. Elizabeth was especially concerned with the poor and the sick, and she began the first free Catholic school in the U.S. Though Elizabeth's life took many twists and turns, she always looked to God for guidance, and she founded the first American religious order for women.

Prayer: God whose ways are not our ways, we thank you for people like St. Elizabeth Ann Seton, who valued following you above all else. When obstacles are placed in our path, we have only to look to people like Mother Seton for an example of courage in the face of adversity. Give us strength of spirit, like her, so that we, too, will recognize your hand in all the events of our lives.

Inspired by Mother Seton's blazing of new paths, help us, Lord, to fearlessly answer your call to begin new ventures that lead others to you. We ask your special blessing on those of us who, like Mother Seton, are entrusted with the formation of young people.

Just as Mother Seton juggled raising her children with the needs of her community, we who are parents seek your grace to balance our families and our ministries. Help us to recognize that you seek not perfection from us, but the desire to do the best we can within the confines of our time and energy.

With admiration for Elizabeth Ann Seton's commitment to you, O Lord, we pray that you will enable us to do the work you have asked us to do.

All of this we ask in the name of Jesus, our Lord. Amen.

Rev. Dr. Martin Luther King, Jr.

Third Monday in January

*In the last days it will be, God declares, that I will pour out
my Spirit upon all flesh, and your sons and your daughters
shall prophesy, and your young men shall see visions,
and your old men shall dream dreams.*

Acts 2:17

Meditation: Martin Luther King, Jr.'s dream lives on when we insist on treating all our brothers and sisters, no matter their skin color or ethnic heritage, with dignity and respect. Dr. King tried to live his life by Jesus' injunction in Matthew 7 to "do to others as you would have them do to you." Wherever there is dehumanization, wherever people are belittled or devalued, Dr. King's dream of freedom and justice can remind us that equality among all people is also God's dream for humanity.

Prayer: Loving God, who looks into the hearts of all people, guide us to work toward Martin Luther King's vision of inclusivity and nondiscrimination for all people. We do not know how to love as we should, and we need your grace to open our hearts to others, especially those who are different from us in any way.

Teach us to forgive those who, because of their own ignorance and woundedness, do us harm, and may we not perpetuate this cycle of injustice. Inspired by Dr. King's goal to love others as Jesus loved, help us to reach out to the poor, the sick, and the homeless, as we try to carry out Jesus' mission here on earth.

May we cry out against violence of any kind as we try to be people of peace, both in our personal and in our professional lives. May Martin's example of nonviolent resistance to evil continue to be a beacon of hope for many generations to come.

This we pray in the name of Jesus, our Savior and Lord. Amen.

St. Paul

January 25, conversion • June 29, with St. Peter

For I am convinced that neither death, nor life, nor angels,
nor rulers, nor things present, nor things to come, nor powers,
nor height, nor depth, nor anything else in all creation, will be
able to separate us from the love of God in Christ Jesus our Lord.

Romans 8:38–39

Meditation: In the history of Christianity, few people have preached the Good News more fervently than Paul. In spite of several imprisonments and persecution, he persevered in evangelizing about Jesus to communities all over Asia Minor and even Europe in the early years of Christianity. The treasure of Paul's faith, wisdom, and theological insights have been imparted to us through his epistles, or letters.

Prayer: Loving God, we thank you for choosing St. Paul as your instrument to share the profound effects of his conversion and his belief in Jesus' saving power. In every age you choose special people to do your work. Help us to respond as passionately as Paul did to your invitation to be disciples of Jesus.

When we need encouragement, we need only turn to Paul's writings in his letters to be strengthened and encouraged by his faith in Christ. Help us in turn to strengthen and encourage others by our own convictions about the love of God found in Jesus.

May we remember that we spread your love not only by our words, but mostly through our actions. Give us the grace to be faithful people of integrity like St. Paul, consistent in our thoughts, words, and deeds.

Inspired by Paul's spirit of inclusivity, we ask that our love for you be far-reaching and embracing of all peoples and nationalities. May we never turn away from brothers or sisters whose outward appearance or beliefs are different from our own.

This we pray in the name of Christ Jesus, our Lord. Amen.

St. Patrick

March 17

The LORD sets prisoners free; the LORD opens the eyes of the blind.
The LORD lifts up those who are bowed down;
the LORD loves the righteous.

Psalm 146:7–8

Meditation: Most of us know St. Patrick as the patron saint of the Irish, but if we were to read a little about his life, we would also recognize that he was a great missionary and evangelizer. All of us are called to witness Christ's love by our words and by our actions. As St. Patrick helped the spread of Christianity in the early Church, he is an example of faithfulness to Jesus' teachings in the midst of difficult circumstances. Also, since he devoted himself to prayer during his active life of ministry, he shows us the importance of this spiritual practice as well.

Prayer: Many of us find it difficult, O Lord, to find a balance between action and contemplation, between faithful ministry and prayerful solitude. Teach us to be like St. Patrick as we strive to keep in mind the importance of prayer in the midst of our service.

May our belief in Jesus' love for all people show itself in how we treat others. May we always be willing, like St. Patrick, to stand up for our belief in the primacy of love.

For all who know what it's like to be separated from loved ones as St. Patrick was in his captivity, may we, like Patrick, hold fast to our knowledge of God's faithful presence. Help us to be examples of joyful perseverance, as St. Patrick was, even when we find it hard to be hopeful.

Help us to teach others about you, O God, by our example of faithful service to your people.

We ask these things in the name of Jesus, your Son and our brother. Amen.

St. Joseph

March 19

*An angel of the Lord appeared to Joseph in a dream and said,
"Get up, take the child and his mother, and flee to Egypt, and
remain there until I tell you; for Herod is about to search for the
child, to destroy him." Then Joseph got up, took the child and
his mother by night, and went to Egypt.*

Matthew 2:13–14

Meditation: We know little about Joseph, the husband of Mary, other
than he was "a righteous man" (Matthew 1:19), which means he
was morally upright, or someone we can look up to. In this day
and age when many find it difficult to keep their commitments,
Joseph's faithful protection of Mary and Jesus reminds us of the
importance of integrity and the willingness to do the right thing.

Prayer: Loving God, we marvel at your foresight in choosing Joseph
to be the husband of Mary. We stand in admiration of his willingness to obey you in difficult circumstances.

Teach us to be like Joseph when we lack the courage to do what
is right. Help us to remember the importance of listening to your
guidance, especially in times of uncertainty.

May we look to St. Joseph for help when we need an example
of what it means to be a good parent. As Joseph shows us by his
life of fatherly protection, may our faithful actions speak louder
than our words.

Especially for all who are stepfathers or adoptive fathers, Joseph
is a witness of selfless love and devotion. Just as Joseph did with
Jesus, help us in the midst of our busy lives to always make our
children and their needs a priority.

All of this we ask in the name of Jesus, our Lord. Amen.

St. Catherine of Siena

April 29

In the same way, let your light shine before others, so that they may see your good works and give glory to your Father in heaven.

Matthew 5:16

Meditation: Catherine of Siena, who lived in Italy in the fourteenth century, was known for her holiness and her preaching. Many people were attracted to her goodness and followed her way of life, which included giving to the poor and taking care of the sick. Catherine traveled and wrote letters in an effort to promote peace in Italy. She is most known for her work *The Dialogue*, a book that recounts her conversations with God.

Prayer: God of holiness, you sent Catherine of Siena in a time when the Christian Church needed people unafraid to speak the truth. Teach us, like Catherine, to live in accordance with your justice and love, so that we, too, may witness what it means to follow Christ.

Inspired by Catherine, may we never give up our efforts to advocate for the poor and helpless, and may we so immerse ourselves in your love that our example encourages others to walk in your ways.

Help us to be people of prayer and remember that we can do nothing without your grace. Allow your spirit to influence and embolden us so that, like Catherine, we can work for peace.

Encourage us not to falter when the results of our ministry are not so easy to see. Most importantly, may we work not for our own recognition and success, but to make you more visible in the world.

May we be people of humility, like Catherine, who use our gifts for the sake of your people. Help us recognize that everyone has something of value to offer, and all should be treated with the dignity they deserve.

We pray these things in the name of your Son, Jesus. Amen.

St. Anthony of Padua

June 13

Or what woman having ten silver coins, if she loses one of them, does not light a lamp, sweep the house, and search carefully until she finds it? When she has found it, she calls together her friends and neighbors, saying, "Rejoice with me, for I have found the coin that I had lost." Just so, I tell you, there is joy in the presence of the angels of God over one sinner who repents.

Luke 15:8–10

Meditation: Anthony of Padua, known popularly as the patron saint of lost articles, was born in Portugal but spent most of his life in Italy. He died in 1231 and was canonized a saint only a year after his death. Anthony, who was a Franciscan and a contemporary of Francis of Assisi, was known for his preaching.

Prayer: Lord God, in St. Anthony we have a wonderful witness of one who was devoted to you and who loved holy Scripture. Teach us to live as people of the word who, like Anthony, show others the way by our love. May we touch the lives of those who, for whatever reason, have lost their faith in you and thus help to restore in them hope for the future.

Give us an appreciation for that which is simple, and help us to know that we are called to stand up for all that which is right and true. Strengthen our conviction to serve you by helping us put our gifts to work for the sake of your people.

Saint Anthony was said to have caused many miracles in his lifetime. Help us to always remember that with you, there is a way out of any darkness or trouble, and that we only need to call upon you for help.

This we pray in the name of your loving Son and our Lord, Jesus. Amen.

St. Ignatius of Loyola

July 31

*Thus says the LORD: Stand at the crossroads, and look,
and ask for the ancient paths, where the good way lies;
and walk in it, and find rest for your souls.*

Jeremiah 6:16

Meditation: Saint Ignatius of Loyola was the founder of the Society of Jesus, or the Jesuits. He was born in Spain in 1491 and experienced a profound conversion in 1521 while recovering from an injury sustained in battle. Ignatius was especially gifted with the art of spiritual direction, and wrote what is known as *The Spiritual Exercises* to help others with the practice of discernment in their spiritual journeys.

Prayer: Loving God, just as you guided Ignatius to become the holy saint that he was, guide us also along the paths that lead to you. Many are the stumbling blocks that impede our growth to become the people you have called us to be. Help us to focus not so much on our failings, but on your grace that sustains us throughout our lives.

May we, like Ignatius, always seek to do your will, and may we learn to reflect well as we face the many choices that make up our days. Strengthen our resolve to make the well-being of your people our first priority as we in turn nurture our spirits through daily prayer.

We ask that we who are educators always put you at the forefront of our learning, just as Ignatius did. Help us to be responsible stewards of your truth so that those we are entrusted to teach will be shaped and molded by your goodness they see in us.

Give us the gift of courage so we may remain steadfast in the midst of the challenges that face us. Guide us to be people of love whose main desire is to see your face in the people we serve.

We pray these things in the name of Christ, our Lord. Amen.

St. Teresa Benedicta of the Cross

Edith Stein, August 9

*Blessed are those who trust in the L*ORD*, whose trust is the L*ORD*.*
They shall be like a tree planted by water, sending out its roots
by the stream. It shall not fear when heat comes, and its leaves
shall stay green; in the year of drought it is not anxious,
and it does not cease to bear fruit.

Jeremiah 17:7–8

Meditation: Edith Stein was born Jewish in Poland, briefly became an atheist, and then studied and taught philosophy in Germany. Later she converted to Catholicism and then became a Carmelite nun. During the years preceding World War II, she wrote a letter to the pope denouncing the Nazi regime. She was killed in a gas chamber at the Auschwitz concentration camp in 1942 and was pronounced a saint by Pope John Paul II in 1998.

Prayer: God of all peoples, we honor the life of Edith Stein, a woman who lived a life of integrity and faithful witness to you in a time of great turmoil. Though we falter sometimes in the strength of our convictions, help us to lead lives worthy of your calling. Like Edith Stein, we ask that we may always put our gifts to use in the building of your kingdom.

Bless us with the ability to accept peoples from all different backgrounds and the courage to denounce racism whenever we encounter it. In a world that cries out for your peace, may we be instruments of reconciliation. Most of all, Lord, we ask for an end to hatred in all its forms as we pray for the grace, like Edith Stein, to stand for love.

We thank you for the gift of this modern saint, who by her life shows us how to stand up for what we believe is right. Help us to embrace our own burdens or crosses and to see that they are paths to you and not impediments.

All this we pray in the name of Jesus, our Lord. Amen.

St. Clare

August 11

[Jesus] said to his disciples, "Therefore I tell you, do not worry about your life, what you will eat, or about your body, what you will wear. For life is more than food, and the body more than clothing."

Luke 12:22–23

Meditation: We have much to learn from Clare of Assisi, follower of Francis and founder of the Poor Clares. She rejected a life of wealth and ease to follow her heart's true desire, which was to become more like Jesus and to live in community with other like-minded women. Clare shows us that the road to happiness lies not in material possessions but in living the values of the Gospel.

Prayer: Loving God, we are thankful for the many the holy women and men who inspire us to live more like Jesus. In a world fraught with violence, we look to gentle Clare as an example of how to live in peace with others.

Ever humble, she inspired Francis and others with her simplicity and devotion to prayer. May we who lead such complicated lives aspire to Clare of Assisi's singleness of heart so that, like her, we may recognize what is truly important. Help us to make prayer a priority in our lives so that we, too, may become more loving individuals.

So much in our society competes for our attention, and we find it difficult to place our focus on you, loving God. Give us the courage to shed all that keeps us scattered and aimless, and help us to turn to what is truly important: loving others as we are loved by you.

Like Clare, make us ever mindful of the materially poor, as well as the poor in spirit, so that we may learn true generosity to those less fortunate than ourselves.

All this we ask in the name of Jesus, your Son and our Lord. Amen.

St. Maximilian Kolbe

August 14

We are afflicted in every way, but not crushed; perplexed, but not driven to despair; persecuted, but not forsaken; struck down, but not destroyed; always carrying in the body the death of Jesus, so that the life of Jesus may also be made visible in our bodies.

2 Corinthians 4:8–10

Meditation: Maximilian Kolbe was a Polish Franciscan priest who was imprisoned in 1941 at Auschwitz concentration camp, and who died that same year by offering his life in place of a fellow prisoner. He is also known for his devotion to Mary the Mother of Jesus, and during his lifetime he promoted veneration to Mary. Franciszek Gajowniczek, the man who Maximilian saved by offering to die in his place, lived until age 94.

Prayer: God of love and forgiveness, the life and death of Maximilian Kolbe shows us there are heroes in every age, and we are grateful for the love and courage he showed by freely choosing to die so that another might live. As Jesus said, "No one has greater love than this, to lay down one's life for one's friends" (John 15:13).

Inspired by his example of selflessness, lead us to love others as fully as Maximilian Kolbe did, so that we may choose like he did to respond to hatred and evil with forgiveness and kindness. Our world desperately needs leaders who are unafraid to stand up for what is right. Teach us what is good and true so that others may also learn from us truth and goodness.

May our love be so far-reaching as to embrace all peoples, including those of different nationalities, races, and religions. May our choices always be made in freedom and peace as was Maximilian Kolbe's, and may we, like him, shine like beacons of hope when the world is full of darkness.

We pray all this in the name of Jesus, your beloved Son. Amen.

Blessed Teresa of Calcutta

September 5

If you remove the yoke from among you, the pointing of the finger,
the speaking of evil, if you offer your food to the hungry and
satisfy the needs of the afflicted, then your light shall rise
in the darkness and your gloom be like the noonday.

Isaiah 58:9–10

Meditation: Many things compete for our attention in the complex world we live in, and many of us feel frazzled by juggling multiple time commitments. By her life, Mother Teresa showed us another way: a way of simplicity, in which she made Jesus her first priority. Devoted to the poor and the dying, Blessed Teresa of Calcutta demonstrated great love, and the process to have her canonized a saint is in motion.

Prayer: Loving God, you show us your face in the lives of people like Blessed Teresa of Calcutta. In a leap of faith, she left her convent life to minister to the poorest of the poor in India. Her single-hearted determination to answer your call to serve others makes her a model of discipleship to the world.

We, too, are called to answer your invitation to serve others, to be the hands and feet of Christ in a world that cries out in need. Give us the strength to answer your call, and help us to remain steadfast during those days and times that are particularly challenging.

Make of us people of prayer, humble to do your will, so that we may receive the grace to do your work. Help us to be especially attentive to those who, for whatever reason, feel unwanted and unloved, as it was to these people that Mother Teresa directed her attention.

In the midst of our ministry, may we never forget that we ourselves are loved by you, for only in remembering that we are your sons and daughters can we love others like Mother Teresa did.

We pray these things through Christ, our Lord. Amen.

St. Gabriel the Archangel

September 29

The angel Gabriel was sent by God to a town in Galilee called Nazareth, to a virgin engaged to a man whose name was Joseph, of the house of David. The virgin's name was Mary. And he came to her and said, "Greetings, favored one! The Lord is with you."

Luke 1:26–28

Meditation: The angel Gabriel is known to us as a messenger of God, one who communicates to humans God's intent. Thus he is recorded as speaking to both Zechariah and to Mary in the book of Luke to announce the impending births of Jesus and John the Baptist. Gabriel is considered the patron saint of communication workers.

Prayer: God of heaven and earth, you sent the angel Gabriel to announce the birth of Jesus to Mary, thus inviting her to a new way of being. Help us to listen and respond to your messengers of truth, those who call us to transformation for the sake of your Son, Jesus.

In this age of mass communication and social media, help us to remember that some of the most important conversations still take place face to face. Mindful of Gabriel's role to convey your plans for humanity, may we also never lose sight of the fact that you use us, too, to speak of your love and your salvation to others.

Remind us to call upon our own guardian angels when we are in need of sustenance. Help us to be angels of hope to all those who are downtrodden and discouraged.

God of all, may we never lose sight of the fact that your ways are not our ways, and may we have the grace to be continually surprised by your intervention in our lives. Help us to trust that you are ever ready and willing to help us when we call upon you.

We ask these things in the name of your Son, Jesus. Amen.

St. Michael the Archangel

September 29

And war broke out in heaven; Michael and his angels fought against the dragon. The dragon and his angels fought back, but they were defeated, and there was no longer any place for them in heaven.

Revelation 12:7–8

Meditation: Many different traditions hold Michael the Archangel in high esteem: Jewish, Muslim and Christian. He is revered as the highest of all the angels, and his name means "who is like to God." Michael is seen as a protector for police officers and can help us in our daily struggles to do good and not harm.

Prayer: Creator God of heaven and earth, you have given us a mighty ally in Michael, your archangel. Tradition tells us that Michael is the highest of your angels and patron of the Christian Church. May we strive to be more like Michael and hold dear the principles of justice and truth.

Many are the conflicts with which we struggle, O God, and we look to St. Michael to help us in our spiritual battles: those against addiction and anything that does not lead us to you. Help us to know, loving God, that you are always with us no matter what challenges we face.

As Michael is said to have overthrown the evil one, help us, Lord, to cast out whatever is sinful in our own lives so we may come ever closer to you. Give us strength, Lord, to overcome our temptations toward selfishness and, instead, instill in us an attitude of love for all.

Just as Michael leads the choirs of angels who praise God, may our lives always serve to praise you, O Lord, as we seek to build your kingdom here on earth.

All this we pray in the name of Jesus. Amen.

St. Thérèse of Lisieux

October 1

For all who are led by the Spirit of God are children of God…
When we cry, "Abba! Father!" it is that very Spirit bearing witness
with our spirit that we are children of God, and if children,
then heirs, heirs of God and joint heirs with Christ.

Romans 8:14, 15–17

Meditation: Thérèse of Lisieux believed that to achieve intimacy with God, one must become humble. Rather than trusting in her own abilities, Thérèse relied on the grace of God to transform and help her. Though some days it might be hard to believe our lives make a difference, we can be inspired by the life of Thérèse, who sought to be like a child, and in her "little way," achieved greatness.

Prayer: So often, Lord, we measure our worth by what we do rather than who we are. We forget that we are your beloved children and that you have called us by name and we are yours. Help us to be more like Thérèse of Lisieux, who found her true value by recognizing how much you loved her.

Inspired by your vision of who we truly are, we can do wonderful things, O Lord, but only with your help. We pray for your grace to carry out all the small, mundane things that make up our days. Doing your work is sometimes hard: Help us to be patient with ourselves and with others when we are discouraged.

May we treat all with whom we come in contact with loving kindness no matter who they are. Like Thérèse, may we show graciousness to everyone, even those who forget to treat us with respect. Help us remember that everyone carries a burden, and we are called to lighten others' loads with our kindness, not to make others' burdens heavier with our irritability.

We pray these things in the name of Jesus, your Son and our Lord. Amen.

St. Francis of Assisi

October 4

Rejoice in the Lord always; again I will say, Rejoice. Let your gentleness be known to everyone. The Lord is near. Do not worry about anything, but in everything by prayer and supplication with thanksgiving let your requests be made known to God.

Philippians 4:4–6

Meditation: Francis of Assisi lived in simplicity and in love and inspires us to do the same. Though born to wealth, he left everything behind to follow Christ. Wholehearted in his desire for truth and goodness, he had a huge impact on the people of his time and was canonized shortly after his death.

Prayer: Loving God, teach me to trust as Francis did so I may learn not to worry about that which is trivial but instead focus on that which is important: loving others as we are loved.

Just as Francis welcomed all he met, may all whom I encounter feel comfortable in my presence. Help me adopt an attitude of acceptance toward everyone and thus be an instrument of your grace to others.

May I remember that true strength lies in gentleness of spirit, and like Francis, may I strive for peace in all my relationships. May the virtue of humility be the foundation of all that I do, and may I not seek after my own glory but only to be of authentic service to others.

Instill in me a reverence for all creation so I, like Francis, may witness to others respect for the beauty of nature and of animals. Let me take into account the fragile nature of this earth so I may help protect its resources for generations to come.

Help my demeanor be one of joy and of gratitude for all you have given me. All this I pray in the name of Jesus, my brother and friend. Amen.

St. Teresa of Jesus of Ávila

October 15

Therefore confess your sins to one another,
and pray for one another, so that you may be healed.
The prayer of the righteous is powerful and effective.

James 5:16

Meditation: We can learn much about prayer from St. Teresa of Ávila, as this is the spiritual devotion for which she is most known. Teresa, with all her imperfections and yet all her saintliness, is an example to all who long to become closer to God and don't know where to begin. Despite encountering fierce opposition to her efforts to reform her Carmelite order, Teresa persevered in faith and good humor, thus showing us determination in the face of great difficulties.

Prayer: Many of us find excuses not to pray in the midst of our busy lives. We say we don't have time or that we are too tired. We fail to realize that our efforts to pray give us the grace we need to survive. Help us to recognize, O God, that you are the source and center of all that we do, and that without you we are nothing.

Sometimes, Lord, we do not get answers to our prayers and we may lose heart. Sometimes it is difficult to see you at work as we face our daily challenges. As you did with Teresa of Ávila, show us your presence in the midst of our circumstances, and thus give us the courage we need to keep going.

Those of us who are doing the work of ministry can look to Teresa for inspiration, as she knew that by our service to others we continue Jesus' mission of love here on earth. Confirm in us, O God, your call to do good as we seek to minister in your name.

We pray these things through Christ, our Lord. Amen.

St. Jude

October 28

But you, beloved, build yourselves up on your most holy faith;
pray in the Holy Spirit; keep yourselves in the love of God;
look forward to the mercy of our Lord Jesus Christ
that leads to eternal life.

Jude 20–21

Meditation: St. Jude was one of Jesus' 12 disciples, and he is known as the patron saint of lost causes. He is a reminder to us that all things are possible with God, and that we are called upon to be people of hope no matter our circumstances. "Now hope that is seen is not hope. For who hopes for what is seen? But if we hope for what we do not see, we wait for it with patience." (Romans 8:24-25)

Prayer: Loving God, we celebrate the life of St. Jude as one who ministered alongside you as one of your disciples. We ask that St. Jude intercede for us on our behalf, he who is one with you in the communion of saints.

May we always remember to turn to you in our need, Lord, since you've promised to be with us forever. Help us to never give in to despair, for to do so is to turn our backs on you.

In this imperfect world of ours, help us to be signs of encouragement and strength to the people around us. Enable us to look past external appearances and to see the hearts of those we serve, especially those whose needs have too long been ignored.

We never know how much a smile or a kind word can lift the spirits of one who needs support. Likewise, we are grateful for those people in our own lives whose care for us helps to keep us going. We know we are called to be in communion with you and with each other.

Mindful of this, we pray these things in the name of your Son and our Savior, Jesus. Amen.

St. Martin de Porres

November 3

The mouths of the righteous utter wisdom,
and their tongues speak justice. The law of their God
is in their hearts; their steps do not slip.

Psalm 37:30–31

Meditation: Martin de Porres, a lay Dominican who lived from 1579 to 1639, had special compassion for the sick and was known for his healing ministry. Those who work in health care can be inspired by Martin de Porres' life as we care for those who are injured or ill. Martin's life helps us recognize that all work, no matter how menial, that is performed with love is important.

Prayer: God of justice and equality, help us learn to live lives of service and love through the example of people like St. Martin de Porres, who reached out to all different kinds of people. May we recognize, like Martin, that you are present in all to whom we minister, and help us to fulfill our duties, even the boring and tedious ones, with humility and grace.

Our world is in great need of people like Martin, whose gentle spirit and charitable actions spoke of a life rooted in God. Help us to be people of prayer, Lord, who always turn to you in our need, and who seek your wisdom as we work for the good of your people.

Martin knew that people of all different backgrounds need love. Help us to see the true nature of the people we serve and to remember that you created all of us in your image and likeness. Give us the courage to stand up for what is right, though our actions may not always be popular or appreciated.

Most of all, Lord, help us to put you at the forefront of all we do, as we seek to live out your concern for the poor, the downtrodden, and the sick.

All this we ask in the name of Jesus. Amen.

Celebrating
Liturgical Seasons

Advent

Preparing Ourselves for Jesus

A voice cries out: "In the wilderness prepare the way of the
LORD, make straight in the desert a highway for our God.
Every valley shall be lifted up, and every mountain and hill
be made low."

Isaiah 40:3–4

Meditation: As we begin the season of Advent, we are challenged to look inside to prepare ourselves for the birth of Christ, even as all around us we witness the commercialism of our society's celebration of Christmas. Advent is a time for stillness and quiet, a time to remind ourselves that we are readying ourselves for Jesus to come to us.

Prayer: Loving God, we are so grateful that you love us so much that you wanted to be one of us in the person of Jesus. Just as he was born in Bethlehem more than 2,000 years ago, we long for Jesus to be born in our hearts this Advent season.

Help us to open our hearts and our minds to your coming, O Lord, and give us the grace to slow down to reflect on where we need you most in our lives. May we remember, Jesus, that you came to us as a baby in weakness and in vulnerability, and so it is in our weakness and vulnerability that we receive you.

As we ready ourselves for you, Lord, we are mindful that sometimes our own lives resemble a wilderness, a land uninhabited by you. You bring new life, new opportunities to the deserts of our hearts, and for this we thank you.

Jesus, we pray that we may help make you incarnate in our midst by our caring words and actions. Likewise, open our eyes to your presence in the people we are called to serve in your name. Wherever there is goodness and love, you are there.

We ask these things in the name of Jesus, who is with us now and forever. Amen.

Prayer for Patience

We wait for new heavens and a new earth, where righteousness is at home. Therefore, beloved, while you are waiting for these things... regard the patience of our Lord as salvation.

2 Peter 3:13–15

Meditation: Most of us are not very good at being patient. We live in an age where an endless supply of information is available at our fingertips, and delayed gratification is an antiquated notion. Even our prayers to God can reflect our impatience with our situation or what we feel we lack. Jesus calls us again and again to patience, for he modeled patience to his disciples, and he is patient with us.

Prayer: Loving God, we come before you in this season of Advent and always to pray for the gift of patience as we wait for you to come to us anew.

Fill out hearts with the steadfast knowledge that you are available to us in our need, that all we have to do is call upon you, and you are there.

May we witness your faithful love to everyone we encounter this day. We ask for the grace to "bear with one another" (Colossians 3:13) as we wait for Jesus to be made manifest in our hearts and in our lives.

Remind us, Lord, that what you have in store for us is usually better than what we could have dreamed of for ourselves. Help us to surrender ourselves to your time table, for we know that your ways are not our ways.

Grow in us the ability to also be patient with ourselves, Lord, knowing that we have to be ready for you to do your work in us. Likewise, we ask for the ability to trust that you do, indeed, have a plan for our lives, and that you long to bring us closer to you.

We pray these things in the name of your Son, Jesus, our Lord. Amen.

Celebrating Joyful Hope

By the tender mercy of our God, the dawn from on high will break upon us, to give light to those who sit in darkness and in the shadow of death, to guide our feet into the way of peace.

Luke 1:78–79

Meditation: Advent is a time when we joyfully anticipate the birth of Jesus. As we wait patiently for his coming, we wonder: How will Jesus make his presence known to us this Christmas season? What blessings lie in store for us—those for which we have longingly prayed, or those which our hearts cannot yet imagine? We know that whatever way Jesus will come to us, it will only be for good and we are grateful.

Prayer: God of abundance, we come to you with open hands as we wait for the birth of your Son, Jesus. Guide us in your ways of love as we prepare our hearts for his coming. Help us to pay attention to the stirrings of our spirits, for you speak to us in quiet ways.

Remind us that we witness to your presence in ways we do not always see, and give us the strength to respond positively to your people. As we minister in your name, help us to be mindful that the glory of your coming is reflected in us this Advent season.

We ask for the grace to forgive whoever may have harmed us so we may wait for Jesus' coming unfettered by the chains of our past hurts. Likewise, give us the grace to ask forgiveness of those we may have harmed so we may lay our burdens down as we ready ourselves for Christmas.

Along with the shepherds and wise men of old, we joyfully anticipate the birth of Jesus with quiet expectation and with wonder and excitement, and we pray that all will receive him in love and in peace.

All this we ask in the name of our Savior, Jesus. Amen.

And the Word Became Flesh

Let the same mind be in you that was in Christ Jesus, who,
though he was in the form of God, did not regard equality
with God as something to be exploited, but emptied himself,
taking the form of a slave, being born in human likeness.

Philippians 2:5–7

Meditation: We pause in wonder to consider the miracle of the In-carnation of Jesus. Jesus becoming human speaks of God's longing to be close to us. The Incarnation of Jesus also lets us know that God truly understands what it means to be human. What better way for God to show us we are loved than to become one of us!

Prayer: God of heaven and earth, we thank you for the gift of your Son, Jesus, for whom we are preparing this Advent season. We are awed and humbled that you took on human likeness in the person of Jesus.

Help us to see just how much you love us, and let us never take the magnitude of your love for granted. Your coming to us as a helpless baby signifies your willingness to be vulnerable and shows us that you long for intimacy with us, not power and dominance.

Lord, teach us to be like Jesus in all that we say and do. Let us be people of love and forgiveness, not hate and resentment. We have so much to learn, Lord, about what it means to be happy. Show us that the path to peace lies in following the ways of your Son, Jesus.

As we ready ourselves to celebrate with joy the birth of Jesus, we ask that you help us bring your people one step closer to the truth of your love for us. Renew in our hearts and in the hearts of those to whom we minister that Jesus is with us now and forever.

This we pray in the name of your beloved Son, Jesus. Amen.

Christmas

The Twelve Days of Christmas

And the Word became flesh and lived among us, and we have seen
his glory, the glory as of a father's only son, full of grace and truth.
From his fullness we have all received, grace upon grace.

John 1:14, 16

Meditation: The twelve days of Christmas is the time between Christmas Day and the day before Epiphany and has been celebrated in different ways by different cultures. For many people around the world, it is a time to continue gift giving and celebrating the birth of Jesus.

December 25: The **birth of our Lord and Savior, Jesus Christ**, who, though divine, came to the world in human form.

December 26: The feast of **St. Stephen**, the first martyr of the Christian Church.

December 27: The feast of **St. John the Evangelist**, the beloved disciple of Jesus and one of the few who stayed at the cross until Jesus' death.

December 28: The feast of the **Holy Innocents,** the children under age two in Bethlehem who, after hearing of Jesus' birth, were murdered by King Herod.

December 29: The feast of **St. Thomas Becket**, who was martyred by followers of King Henry II in Canterbury Cathedral in London.

December 30: The feast of the **Holy Family**, a model for Christian families everywhere.

December 31: The feast of **St. Sylvester**, an early pope of the church.

January 1: The **Solemnity of Mary, the Holy Mother of God**, who lovingly cared for Jesus, her Son.

January 2: The feast of **Sts. Basil the Great and Gregory Nanzianzen**, monks in the early church who fought the heresy of Arianism, or the belief that Jesus was not divine.

January 3: The feast of the **Most Holy Name of Jesus, the Son of God**, who was sent to "save his people from their sins" (Matthew 1:21). Jesus is also known as "Emmanuel," which means, "God is with us" (Matthew 1:23).

January 4: The feast of **St. Elizabeth Ann Seton**, the founder of the first religious community of women in the U.S.

January 5: The feast of **St. John Neumann**, a founder of Catholic education in the U.S.

Prayer: Loving God, we are grateful for you and your saints during this special Christmastime. We ask for the grace to model our lives after you and to nurture the virtues and values they demonstrate. We pray this in Jesus' name. Amen.

The True Meaning of the Christmas Season

But the angel said to them, "Do not be afraid; for see—
I am bringing you good news of great joy for all the people:
to you is born this day in the city of David a Savior,
who is the Messiah, the Lord."

Luke 2:10–11

Meditation: We human beings are easily distracted, and many things get in the way of remembering that each Christmas we celebrate the truth of God's great love for us. Just as Jesus was born 2,000 years ago, so is he born in our hearts again each Christmas. This Christmas season, let us pause to celebrate the gift of God's great love for us by giving us Jesus.

Prayer: Loving God, teach us that after we have unwrapped our presents, eaten our Christmas dinner, and opened our cards, that one thing remains: your love for us. Help us to always remember that, first and foremost, it is your love we celebrate this Christmas season.

We pray that we may show your love to others, not just during the Christmas season, but always. Help us to slow down enough to recognize the many ways you are present to us as we continue to celebrate the birth of your Son, Jesus.

May our actions further the ways of peace, and may our kindness communicate your love. Melt away the grudges against others we carry in our hearts, and forgive us for the times we fail you and those for whom we care.

Enkindle your hope in us, Lord, that we may be signs of hope to your people this Christmas season. Give us joy so that others will know that, in the gift of your Son, Jesus, there is no room for fear or gloom.

We pray these things in the loving name of Jesus. Amen.

The Epiphany of the Lord

January 6 or the Sunday between January 2–8

*In the time of King Herod, after Jesus was born in Bethlehem
of Judea, wise men from the East came to Jerusalem, asking,
"Where is the child who has been born king of the Jews? For we
observed his star at its rising, and we have come to pay him homage."*

Matthew 2:1–2

Meditation: The feast of the Epiphany is the time during the Christmas season when we celebrate the Magi's visit to the baby Jesus. Along with the three wise men, we mark this special day with joy, for God has seen fit to come to us in the form of a human being, Jesus of Nazareth.

Prayer: Creator of all that is good, on this special day of Epiphany we are privileged to witness the miracle of your presence in our world. We thank you for the gift of your Son, Jesus, who shows how to love and how to live.

Like the wise men, we are "overwhelmed with joy" (Matthew 2:10) as we come together to praise you, God, for coming to us in the person of Jesus. We ask that, in some small way, we may share in the witness of your love for those to whom we are called to minister in your name.

When we are tired and grumpy, we ask for the gifts of patience and perseverance.

When we feel hopeless and alone, we ask that you show us that you are with us always.

When we are called to forgive, we ask for the grace to lay our grievances aside, knowing that we have been forgiven by you.

Instill in us your light and your goodness so we may illuminate the path to you for others. Show us the ways of peace and justice, that with your help we may transform the world in which we live.

We pray all this in the name of our brother and Savior, Jesus. Amen.

Lent

Our Collective Need for Grace

For by grace you have been saved through faith, and this is not your own doing; it is the gift of God—not the result of works, so that no one may boast.

Ephesians 2:8–9

Meditation: Lent is a time when Christians the world over come together to acknowledge our human need for God's grace. All of us are sinners, and—fortunately for us—God loves us in spite of our flaws! In fact, God longs to bring healing to our divisions, both individual and communal, and because of this, we have the courage to bring our needs to the Lord.

Prayer: Loving God, we come before you this Lent with outstretched arms, ready to receive your love and forgiveness. Though you know our needs even before we name them, we call upon you now, Lord of our salvation.

Many are the burdens that we carry, but you, O Lord, will help us carry our loads. Likewise, we ask for the strength and courage to lift others up by offering them encouragement and hope.

Much of our world is torn apart by violence, hunger, and illness. Only you, Lord, can bring unity out of strife, plenty to our want, and healing to our sickness, for you are a God of abundance and love.

Give us courage and faith so we may believe in you always, and may our trust in your providence show your goodness to others. Empty us of whatever separates us from you. Instead, fill us with your mercy, for we long to know your ways.

This Lenten season as we die to our selfishness and sin, Lord, may we rise with you in glory on Easter Sunday.

All of this we pray in the name of our Lord and Savior, Jesus Christ. Amen.

Reconciliation

For you, O LORD, are good and forgiving, abounding in steadfast love to all who call on you. Give ear, O LORD, to my prayer; listen to my cry of supplication. In the day of my trouble I will call on you, for you will answer me.

Psalm 86:5–7

Meditation: All of us need to be reconciled: to God, to one another, and to ourselves. God knows the needs of our hearts and wants to bring wholeness and healing to us. All we have to do is come before the Lord with an open and sincere heart, and the Lord will respond to our desire for forgiveness.

Prayer: God of mercy and compassion, we long to be made new again by the cleansing power of your love. Only you can mend our broken relationships and broken hearts; we need your grace to change our hearts and restore our souls.

No matter what our journey has been, you love us, Lord. You continually call us forth to new life and new beginnings, and we praise you and we thank you.

Help us to bless others with the forgiveness and acceptance we have received from you, O God, for countless lives are broken, and so many hunger to know your love. May all that we say and do help bring about your peace in this world, a world that cries out for your consoling presence.

Most especially, God, help us to teach our children the path to unity and reconciliation so that we may correct the mistakes of the past. Forgive the errors of our ways so we may be recover our former innocence.

Jesus, the way, the truth and the life, we are so grateful for the gift of reconciliation.

We pray in your name that all will know the joy of your salvation. Amen.

The Way of the Cross

*But we do see Jesus, who for a little while was made lower
than the angels, now crowned with glory and honor
because of the suffering of death, so that by the grace of God
he might taste death for everyone.*

Hebrews 2:9

Meditation: Jesus shows us through his death and resurrection that evil does not have the last word; that even when all seems lost, there is always room for hope. Jesus fully embraced all that it means to be human, including death, and by his rising we know that we will have eternal life.

Prayer: Jesus, we honor and glorify you for your tremendous love for us that knows no bounds. We ask that when we feel forlorn and forsaken, we will remember how you trusted God in the Garden of Gethsemane when you said, "Not my will but yours be done" (Luke 22:42).

Give us the strength to always turn to you when our belief in goodness wavers. Help us to be signs of your love and thus bless the people who need reassurance that there is more to life than what meets the eye.

We also pray, Jesus, that through the power of your death and resurrection, we will receive the grace we need not to fear our own death. We pray that knowing our loved ones who have passed are with you will temper our grief for them.

We ask for the strength to accept our own daily crosses, Jesus, as we learn to follow you. Teach us that in dying to ourselves, we will rise with you.

Our world needs to see the power and hope of your resurrection is always present and available to us. May we grow in our ability to witness to your goodness so our ministry to others will be life-giving and transformative.

All this we pray in the holy name of Jesus. Amen.

Jesus

*Therefore God also highly exalted him and gave him the name
that is above every name, so that at the name of Jesus every
knee should bend, in heaven and on earth and under the earth,
and every tongue should confess that Jesus Christ is Lord,
to the glory of God the Father.*

Philippians 2:9–11

Meditation: During this Lenten season, we glorify the holy name of Jesus, whose love for us knows no bounds. We celebrate Jesus' willingness to become like us in all ways except sin, and we thank him for his absolute trust in his Abba, his father, that sustained him even in the midst of his suffering and death.

Prayer: Loving God, we ask for the grace to put on the mind of Christ so that love is the driving force that influences our every thought, word, and action. We are grateful that you have called us to continue Jesus' ministry of compassion and inclusiveness for your people.

Instill in us the desire to follow Jesus always, and may we receive the courage to answer Jesus' invitation to love wholeheartedly and without reserve.

We ask that you will help us to embody Jesus' gentleness and peace in this world that needs your soothing touch. We ask that you will work through us to make Jesus powerfully present so that others will not lose hope.

Help us to be people of prayer so we will become more and more like Jesus. We pray, God, that you will enable us to listen to the "still, small voice within" that longs to guide us in the ways of love and compassion.

Jesus, we long to be people of justice, but sometimes we are afraid. Help us stand up for those who have no voice and give us the strength to restore dignity and respect to all your people.

We ask all this in the holy name of Jesus. Amen.

The Last Supper

I am the vine, you are the branches. Those who abide in me
and I in them bear much fruit, because apart from me
you can do nothing.

John 15:5

Meditation: Even on Jesus' last night with his disciples, he lovingly gave them words of wisdom with which to remember him. Jesus told his disciples, and he tells us, that he needs to be the center of all we say and do. When we unite ourselves with Jesus, our lives bear witness to him and we are productive and useful.

Prayer: Lord, we recognize our need for you and we ask for the grace to unite ourselves to you, for we are nothing without you.

With humility, Jesus, you washed the feet of your disciples at your last supper with them. Teach us humility, too, so we look for ways to serve others and not ourselves.

Jesus' last meal with his disciples was the culmination of his years of healing, teaching, and preaching. Like Jesus, will we be able look back on our ministry to others and know we have given our all?

Give us the courage, Lord, not to be stingy with our love but to wholeheartedly pour ourselves out for your people. May we truly abide in you, Jesus, so that we may be your hands and feet to those we serve.

Help us to always look for your face, Jesus, in those to whom we minister. Likewise, we pray that through our actions of love, others will be able to draw closer to you so we may all abide in you together.

We thank you for the gift of your call to us, and we ask that we may always remember the privilege that is ours to bear fruit in your name.

We pray all these things through Christ, our Lord. Amen.

The Challenge of the Cross

*We proclaim Christ crucified, a stumbling block to Jews
and foolishness to Gentiles, but to those who are the called,
both Jews and Greeks, Christ the power of God and the wisdom
of God. For God's foolishness is wiser than human wisdom,
and God's weakness is stronger than human strength.*

1 Corinthians 1:23–25

Meditation: No one can escape suffering; it is part of the human condition. Yet what is our reaction to our trials? Do we rail against them as we complain bitterly, do we accept them with silent stoicism, or are we somewhere in between those two reactions? By dying on the cross, Jesus fully embraced the eventuality all humans must face, but he also showed us that love and goodness surpass even death.

Prayer: Jesus, we come before you today asking for your grace to deal with the crosses of our lives. You know our hearts and our struggles better than we know ourselves, and you have promised to always be with us.

Teach us that our hardships do not define us and will not have the final word in our lives. Teach us also that you, Jesus, who knows what it's like to suffer and to die, will give us the strength to carry on in the midst of our difficulties.

Enliven our spirits so that we may be beacons of hope to others who face adversity. May we be heartened by your love so that we may encourage and affirm those who need lifting up. Help us also to open our hearts to others' kindness when our own spirits are sagging.

We pray, Jesus, that we may always look to you for guidance when we need support, and not to the standards of this world.

All of this we ask in your holy name. Amen.

Easter

We Are an Easter People

I pray that you may have the power to comprehend, with all
the saints, what is the breadth and length and height and depth,
and to know the love of Christ that surpasses knowledge,
so that you may be filled with all the fullness of God.

Ephesians 3:18–19

Meditation: By his death and resurrection, Jesus has vanquished the power of sin, and so we rejoice. There is no room for darkness and despair in our lives because the power of Jesus' resurrection has conquered all evil. We have only to open ourselves to the mystery of God's love in Jesus to know the hope of salvation that is truly ours, now and forevermore.

Prayer: Jesus, we are humbled by the gift of your love for us. Pour into our hearts the knowledge of the wonder of your rising from the dead. Help us know that, with you by our side, we have no cause for fear.

Jesus, we claim the power of your resurrection as we pray in your name for ourselves and for all your people. We ask that we may always know the grace that is ours to overcome all obstacles if we believe in you.

May we remember that by our baptism, we have been transformed by your Spirit into new life, and called to be your holy people. Help us to recognize your indwelling presence in our hearts, and let our actions reflect the power of your redeeming love.

Since we know you have forgiven us our indiscretions, Lord, help us to reconcile with those who have hurt us in any way.

We pray that we may extend to all we meet the peace that has been given to us in Christ Jesus, and we pray this in his name. Amen.

The Ascension of the Lord

Thursday after the Sixth Sunday or the Seventh Sunday of Easter

*Then he led them out as far as Bethany, and, lifting up his hands,
he blessed them. While he was blessing them, he withdrew from them
and was carried up into heaven. And they worshipped him,
and returned to Jerusalem with great joy, and they were
continually in the temple blessing God.*

Luke 24:50–53

Meditation: Jesus' ascension tells us that he is now and forever with God in heaven, and because of this, he is also with us in a new way. We can count on Jesus to help us no matter what we experience. Jesus' disciples knew he would always be with them as they carried on his mission, and we can take comfort in that Jesus will always be with us, too.

Prayer: Jesus, before your ascension into heaven you charged your disciples to "go into all the world and proclaim the Good News to the whole creation" (Mark 16:15). We are your modern-day disciples, and we, too are called to preach the Gospel to your people by all we say and do.

Help us to call on you for strength as we do your work, and may we remember that our ministry should always point to you and not to ourselves.

May we take joy in the fact that some day we, too, will be with you forever in paradise and reunited with those we love who have gone before us.

Give us the patience and dedication we need to carry on your mission of teaching, healing, and preaching. Help us to see you in those with whom we work, and we ask for the grace to witness your presence as well.

We ask that you remind us that we have been given all we need to do the work of Jesus here on earth, and we pray all these things in Jesus' name. Amen.

Pentecost Sunday

*When the day of Pentecost had come, they were all together
in one place. And suddenly from heaven there came a sound
like the rush of a violent wind....All of them were filled with the
Holy Spirit and began to speak in other languages,
as the Spirit gave them ability.*

Acts 2:1–2, 4

Meditation: In the Gospel of John, Jesus tells his disciples that his Father is sending the Holy Spirit to teach them. On Pentecost, the disciples were filled with Jesus' risen Spirit, and so are we gifted by that same Spirit in our baptism. Wherever goodness happens in the name of Jesus, the Holy Spirit is there. As ministers of Christ, we use the gifts the Spirit has given us to carry on the saving work of Jesus.

Prayer: Holy Spirit, we thank you for your presence in our lives, teaching us, reminding us of God's love and guiding us. Help us to pay attention to your stirrings in our hearts so that we may do God's work and walk in the ways of Jesus.

Jesus, it is your Spirit that calls us forth to minister in your name, and it is your Spirit that sustains us in our ministry. Strengthen our desire to do good for the sake of your people, so that your love may always prevail.

Attune us to the needs of our time, Holy Spirit, so that we can be ready to answer your invitation to heal, to teach, and to work for unity and peace. As Jesus responded to the needs of his followers, help us to respond to those in need.

Holy Spirit, enkindle in us the fire of your love, so we may be signs of your presence in the world.

We pray this in Jesus' name. Amen.

Celebrating
Special Days

Feast Days

The Baptism of the Lord

Sunday after January 6

In those days Jesus came from Nazareth of Galilee and was baptized by John in the Jordan. And just as he was coming up out of the water, he saw the heavens torn apart and the Spirit descending like a dove on him. And a voice came from heaven, "You are my Son, the Beloved; with you I am well pleased."

Mark 1:9–11

Meditation: After Jesus' baptism, God affirmed how loved and how special Jesus was, and this knowledge of his belovedness stayed with him for the rest of his life. It was Jesus' awareness of how loved he was that gave him courage and strength throughout his public ministry and enabled him to love others as he was loved. And so it is with us. The more we get in touch with how truly loved we are by God, the more we are able to love others as God loves us.

Prayer: Jesus, our brother, as we remember your baptism, may we be reminded as you were that we are God's beloved sons and daughters. Help us to soak in our awareness of God's great love for us so that, like you, we may further the kingdom of God here on earth.

Teach us to recognize the "belovedness" of all with whom we come in contact so we may treat everyone with the respect and dignity they deserve.

We thank you for the gift of our own baptism when we received the gift of the Holy Spirit and were welcomed into the community of believers. We ask for the grace to answer your call to feed the hungry, welcome the stranger, clothe the naked, give shelter to the homeless, and heal the sick.

All of this we ask in your holy name. Amen.

Week of Prayer for Christian Unity

January 18–25

The glory that you have given me I have given them,
so that they may be one, as we are one, I in them and you in me,
that they may become completely one, so that the world
may know that you have sent me and have loved them
even as you have loved me.

John 17:22–23

Meditation: One of Jesus' final prayers with his disciples was for unity, a unity based on the knowledge of God's great love for everyone. All across the world we are mindful of Jesus' desire that we may all be one, and this week we echo that desire in our prayer together. Christian unity reflects the notion that all of Jesus' followers share in the truth of the mystery of our redemption.

Prayer: Jesus whose saving grace transforms us all, we pray this week that all Christians may be one, as you and the Father are one. Grant us the freedom and courage to see our commonalities rather than our differences. Help us to focus on our larger purpose, which is to further your mission here on earth.

As Christians work together around the world to serve others in Jesus' name, may we witness to God's love and compassion and thus share the Good News with all humanity. Change our hearts that ours may be a message of peace and justice for all and lead us forward in open dialogue with our brothers and sisters in Christ.

We look forward to a hopeful future where all Christians everywhere share a common purpose: to love each other as they have been loved. Teach us to recognize our need for one another and help us to truly listen to those who share our longing to bring forth God's kingdom.

We ask these things in the name of Jesus, Savior of all. Amen.

The Presentation of the Lord

February 2

When the time came for their purification according to the law of Moses, [Mary and Joseph] brought [Jesus] up to Jerusalem to present him to the Lord (as it is written in the law of the Lord, "Every firstborn male shall be designated as holy to the Lord").

Luke 2:22–23

Meditation: As the Christmas season comes to a close, just as Mary and Joseph presented Jesus to the Lord so many years ago, we also present ourselves to the Lord every time we come together to pray. We are mindful of the ways Jesus has been born in our hearts this past Christmas season, and we are called to remember the joy of the Incarnation all year long.

Prayer: We come before you, Lord, with open minds and hearts, as we celebrate the feast of your presentation in the temple. We ask your blessing this day and all days, as we attempt to witness your love to a world that sorely needs healing. We thank you for the opportunity to show your presence to others through our lives and our ministries.

We ask you to light our way as we pray that you, the Light of the World, will guide us in all our endeavors. Like Simeon and Anna, who recognized who you truly were in your presentation in the Temple, help us recognize you in the people whom we serve.

Purify our intentions to do good, and may our efforts to further your mission always be honest and true. Help us to be people of prayer so our thoughts and words may lead others to you. Give us the grace to say "yes" to you, as Mary did, and to trust in your everlasting faithfulness.

All of this we pray in you holy name. Amen.

The Annunciation of the Lord

March 25

The angel said to her, "Do not be afraid, Mary, for you have found
favor with God. And now, you will conceive in your womb
and bear a son, and you will name him Jesus."

Luke 1:30–31

Meditation: Every time we open our hearts to God we, like Mary, are saying "yes" to the Lord. When we try to be good stewards of our resources, both time and money, when we treat others with kindness, when we maintain a positive attitude—all of these are ways we can say "yes" to God. God continually invites us to be in relationship with God and with each other. How will we respond?

Prayer: Loving God, like the angel Gabriel did with Mary, you come to us in a variety of ways each and every day. We thank you for your presence in our lives and your invitation to draw closer to you.

Mary's yes to you was a profound, history-changing event. Though we often do not see the ramifications of our decisions to do good, we ask that you give us the strength to keep following you.

May the people to whom we minister, who long for a safe refuge in the midst of life's storms, be encouraged by our fidelity to them and to you. Help us to be heralds of hope to your people by our dedication, our thoughtfulness, and our love.

Though we cannot see the fullness of your divine plan at work, help us to trust, like Mary, that you are intimately involved in each of our lives, and that you desire goodness and wholeness for everyone.

We thank you, Lord, for your willingness to come to us in human form in the person of Jesus. Help us to communicate your presence to all with whom we work.

We pray these things in the name of your Son, Jesus. Amen.

National Day of Prayer

First Thursday in May

Your way, O God, is holy. What god is so great as our God?
You are the God who works wonders; you have displayed
your might among the peoples.

Psalm 77:13–14

Meditation: Truly it is a wonderful thing when peoples of all different religions can come together in prayer, for nothing is so unifying as lifting one's heart to God. God the Creator loves us all, and desires that all can live together in peace and harmony. We join with our brothers and sisters from different backgrounds and beliefs to proclaim that God is good and worthy of praise.

Prayer: Source of all goodness, we come together today to ask your blessing for our country and our world. As a nation we need to look to you for guidance and for truth, for we recognize that only with you steering our course can we pursue the principles of justice and freedom.

Transform our hearts to serve you and only you. Transform our communities that they may be safe havens for all. Transform our nation so we can live and work together in peace and thus model to the world what it means to exist in harmony.

We are grateful for the gifts you have bestowed upon us, and we ask that you help us to reach out to those less fortunate than ourselves. We pray that all who seek employment may be rewarded with jobs. We especially ask for an end to hunger and violence, for too many of our children and our neighborhoods are plagued with these evils.

Renew our spirits and our commitment to follow you, O Lord, on this day of prayer. Help us to always make you a priority in our lives, and heal our divisions.

We ask these things in your holy name, dear Lord. Amen.

The Visitation of the Blessed Virgin Mary

May 31

Elizabeth was filled with the Holy Spirit and exclaimed with a loud cry, "Blessed are you among women, and blessed is the fruit of your womb. And why has this happened to me, that the mother of my Lord comes to me?"

Luke 1:41–43

Meditation: Every time we celebrate the gift of new life, we remember how joyfully Elizabeth greeted her cousin Mary when Elizabeth came to visit her. Our own lives are full of new beginnings, new adventures in ministering to God's people to which the Lord invites us. When we assent to God's call to further Jesus' mission, we remember Mary, who said "yes" to God's call to be Jesus' Mother.

Prayer: Loving God, many are the comings and goings in our own lives: there are times we greet joyfully those whom we love, and there are times we sadly bid our loved ones goodbye.

No matter our circumstances, help us to always seek to follow you in our transitions. At the start of a new project or the close of a chapter in our life, let us look to you for courage, guidance and strength.

Like Mary, who humbly proclaimed your greatness in the midst of Elizabeth's praise, we honor and glorify you, Lord, as you summon us to be your instruments in a world that cries out for your presence. We recognize that it is only through your grace that we are able to accomplish the good to which we are called.

We ask that you help us to value not only our own but others' roles in doing your work. In your marvelous plan of salvation, Lord, everyone has been assigned a task to complete. Help us to be like Mary, who models for us what it means to joyfully give her all to you.

We ask this in the name of your Son, Jesus. Amen.

The Transfiguration of the Lord

August 6

*Six days later, Jesus took with him Peter and James and John,
and led them up a high mountain apart, by themselves.
And he was transfigured before them, and his clothes became
dazzling white, such as no one on earth could bleach them.*

Mark 9:2–3

Meditation: All three synoptic Gospels depict Jesus' transfiguration as happening right after his admonition to his disciples that being his follower means taking up one's cross to follow him. One could interpret this to mean that there is no glory without suffering! Though many of us long for "peak moments" in our work lives, whether that means a promotion, a raise, or simply praise from one's supervisor, Jesus' transfiguration is an example that we are transformed when we make God a priority in our lives.

Prayer: God of majesty and light, we humbly come before you today to ask your help in taking up our crosses to minister to your people. Grant us the ability to remember how we have been blessed so we can in turn bless others. Give us patience with ourselves when are tempted to complain about our responsibilities, and help us to always look to you for strength.

Walk with us on the days our burdens are too heavy to carry by ourselves, and help us to recognize that our troubles pale in comparison to the sufferings of some of our brothers and sisters. In our faith-based institution, we are a community, Lord: Help us to share in the sorrows and joys of those with whom we work.

May we always look to Jesus to truly model for us what it means to give freely of ourselves. And may our giving by done with joy and lightness of heart, and never grudgingly or with resentment.

We ask these things in the holy name of Jesus, our Lord. Amen.

All Saints

November 1

The gifts [God] gave were that some would be apostles,
some prophets, some evangelists, some pastors and teacher,
to equip the saints for the work of ministry, for building up
the body of Christ, until all come to the unity of the faith
and of the knowledge of the Son of God, to maturity,
to the measure of the full stature of Christ.

Ephesians 4:11–13

Meditation: How fortunate that we are part of a communion of saints! God's holy people who have gone before us show us how to live. By their example we learn more about how to love and how to pray. We are all called to holiness, to use the gifts with which God has equipped us to build up the body of Christ, and as we do, we discover what it means to experience true joy.

Prayer: God of wisdom and truth, we thank you for the witness of our spiritual ancestors the saints, who demonstrate for us how to live as Jesus did. They are from many countries and from many ages, but they all share in common their love for you and for their neighbors.

Help us to grow into "the measure of the full stature of Christ" by developing our gifts for the sake of your people. Teach us to see and to respond to those persons who most need our attention so we can further Jesus' mission of service and healing.

We remember our loved ones who have gone before us and who are now with you in heaven. Though we mourn their passing, we are comforted by the memories of their time with us on here on earth. Give us the grace to treasure our lives, and may we learn to live every moment of every day until we are fully one with you.

We ask this in the name of Jesus, our Lord. Amen.

Holidays

New Year's Day

January 1

*A new heart I will give you, and a new spirit
I will put within you; and I will remove from your body
the heart of stone and give you a heart of flesh.*

Ezekiel 36:26

Meditation: In the midst of New Year's resolutions and all the festivities that surround this holiday, our God is waiting patiently to draw us closer. We are always free to choose to respond or not to God's invitation to greater intimacy. God uses the people and events of our lives to show us that God is ever present and available to us, and God speaks to us in our hearts if we can become still enough to hear.

Prayer: God of everlasting faithfulness, we greet the beginning of this year with joy and optimism. We ask that this year be a time of new ventures to serve your people better. Guide us with your Spirit that we will make decisions that promote the well-being of those to whom we minister.

We ask that you will enable us to see the face of Jesus in all we encounter this year. We also ask that you give us the ability to stay positive in the midst of challenges. Help us to live our lives and do your work one day at a time, knowing that your strength and presence will always sustain us.

Give us enthusiasm when we falter. Keep us motivated when we are tired. Refresh our spirits when we need to be restored to do your work the best way possible. Remind us when we forget why we are here: because you have called us to help others.

Lord, help us let go of the past and rededicate ourselves to be your hands and your feet in your world.

We ask all of this in the name of your Son, Jesus. Amen.

Valentine's Day

February 14

Love is patient; love is kind; love is not envious or boastful
or arrogant or rude. It does not insist on its own way;
it is not irritable or resentful; it does not rejoice in wrongdoing,
but rejoices in the truth. It bears all things, believes all things,
hopes all things, endures all things.

1 Corinthians 13:4–7

Meditation: Our lives are made richer by the people who love us and who we love. Valentine's Day can be an opportunity to celebrate the friendships we enjoy as well as our romantic relationships. "Beloved, let us love one another, because love is from God; everyone who loves is born of God and knows God" (1 John 4:7).

Prayer: We celebrate love in all its forms on this special day in the middle of winter. We ask especially, Lord, that we can open ourselves to your love for us so we can better love one another.

We pray for all who are alone or feel unloved, that they will feel your presence, Lord, and will be comforted by your love. We pray for the grace to reach out to those who need to be reminded of their belovedness.

Help us to never take anyone's love for granted, and may we always express our gratitude for the ways in which we are loved. Help us remember that love is eternal as we cherish the memories of those we loved who have gone before us.

Give us the ability to recognize that the more we love, the more our lives are enhanced: the gift of love does not diminish us in any way. Give us the courage to love generously and unconditionally as Jesus did, and in doing so may ours and others' lives be transformed.

We pray these things in the name of Jesus. Amen.

Memorial Day

Last Monday in May

But the souls of the righteous are in the hand of God,
and no torment will ever touch them. In the eyes of the foolish
they seemed to have died, and their departure was thought
to be a disaster, and their going from us to be their destruction;
but they are at peace.

Wisdom 3:1–3

Meditation: On Memorial Day, we celebrate those who have served in our country's armed forces and have lost their lives. We are mindful of their bravery and we are grateful for their tremendous sacrifice. The memories of our armed service men and women who have passed will remain forever in our hearts. "No one has greater love than this, to lay down one's life for one's friends" (John 15:13).

Prayer: God of all life, we come to you today to remember the many soldiers who died while serving our country. Together we thank them for their heroism for giving their lives in the line of duty.

We also pray for the families who have been torn apart by the tragedy of war. Though nothing can replace their loved ones who have died, we ask that you watch over the spouses and children of our fallen military personnel.

May your peace triumph over the many conflicts of our world so that some day, war will be no more. Help us to be people of peace, people whose words and actions build others up and do not tear them down, people whose kindness is contagious and whose actions promote harmony.

As we honor the memories of the brave men and women who gave the ultimate sacrifice, that of their lives, help us also to be people of courage as we serve our brothers and sisters in Christ.

We pray these things through Christ, our Lord. Amen.

Independence Day

July 4

*Now the Lord is the Spirit, and where
the Spirit of the Lord is, there is freedom.*

2 Corinthians 3:17

Meditation: Independence Day is not only a day to celebrate the many freedoms we enjoy as Americans, but to thank our forefathers and mothers for the sacrifices they made in building our country. It is also a time to pray for all the people throughout the world who are denied basic human rights because of governmental corruption.

Prayer: God of all peoples, you long for wholeness and dignity for your children. Wherever there is freedom, you are there. Wherever there are equal rights for all citizens, your Spirit is present. We praise you and thank you for the gift of liberty.

We ask that we never take the privilege of our freedom for granted. We pray that we Americans will remember that we are called to be a model of democracy for the rest of the world. Help us find balance, Lord, as we care for our citizens while we care for others all over the globe.

Mindful of Pope Paul VI's admonition that if we want peace, we must work for justice, inspire in us the passion to follow your ways, O Lord, as we seek to do what is fair for all. Open our eyes to the want that is present in our very midst, loving God, so that freedom for everyone will not be a far-off dream but a reality.

If there are chains of sin that bind us, Lord, we ask that we be given the grace to break free. Lead us on the path of conversion and healing so we may learn inner freedom as well. Soften our hearts so that by our love we may call forth others into your freedom, Lord.

We pray these things through Christ, our Lord. Amen.

Labor Day

First Monday in September

Yet you have made [humans] a little lower than God,
and crowned them with glory and honor.
You have given them dominion over the works of your hands;
you have put all things under their feet.

Psalm 8:5–6

Meditation: Labor Day is not only the symbolic end of summer, it is a day in which we celebrate the achievements of workers everywhere. God has given us the gift of work so that we may feel pride in our accomplishments and so that we can contribute to the well-being of others. We thank God for the ability to use our skills and talents for our own and others' good.

Prayer: God the author of all our gifts, part of your call to us to become fully human is to learn work that is meaningful and valuable. Give us the self-awareness and the opportunities to find work that gives us joy and uses our capabilities.

We pray that our work will in some way help to further Jesus' mission here on earth. We ask that you will guide us in our efforts to do work that is fulfilling and that helps others.

We remember those who are disabled physically and emotionally and thus are unable to work. We ask that they can find other ways to contribute the gifts of themselves for the good of others.

As our summer draws to a close, we pray that we may learn the value of being as well as doing. Help us to remember to look for you for strength whenever we feel stressed by the pressures of our work.

Help us to acknowledge the contributions of others as we go about our daily business. Remind us that our work is done best when it is done in community.

We ask these things in the name of your Son, Jesus. Amen.

Halloween

October 31

*And God, who searches the heart, knows what is in the mind
of the Spirit, because the Spirit intercedes for the saints
according to the will of God.*

Romans 8:27

Meditation: Halloween used to be the vigil for All Saints' Day, a time when Christians prayed for their loved ones who had died. Ancient Christians believed this day (All Hallow's Eve) was also a time when souls from purgatory were able to visit their homes on earth. Through the centuries, these beliefs have changed to bring us to our current celebration of Halloween.

Prayer: Creator God, who we are has a lot to do with our ancestors. As we celebrate the silliness of Halloween, we know that soon we will remember all our loved ones who have passed away.

In our society's preoccupation with youth, we shun all talk of death and dying, yet death is an inevitable part of life. Help us to live each moment of each day to its fullest so that we will be less afraid of our end when it comes.

We thank you for our loved ones who, though they are with you for eternity, are still with us in spirit. We remember their love, their memories, and the lessons they taught us while they were still on earth.

As Halloween gives us the opportunity to become like children again, we ask that we can always maintain a joyful attitude about life. We pray that by living positively, we can impact the people we serve in a positive way.

Help us remember, Lord, that with you by our side, we have nothing to fear. "For I am convinced that neither death, nor life, nor angels, nor rulers...will be able to separate us from the love of God in Christ Jesus our Lord" (Romans 8:38–39).

This we pray in the name of Jesus. Amen.

Thanksgiving

Fourth Thursday in November

*It is good to give thanks to the LORD, to sing praises to your name,
O Most High; to declare your steadfast love in the morning,
and your faithfulness by night.*

Psalm 92:1–2

Meditation: It has been said that a thankful heart is a sure-fire way to increase one's blessings. All the more reason to celebrate this special time of year—Thanksgiving! This very special holiday gives us an opportunity to pause and take stock of all God has given us, and to express our heartfelt gratitude to God and each other.

Prayer: Loving God, you have given us innumerable blessings: the gifts of life, love, laughter, friendship, and family. We thank you for the abundance of your blessings to us, especially on this day of Thanksgiving.

As we come together to express our gratitude for all you have bestowed on us, we remember those less fortunate, those who have few blessings to count. We ask that as we celebrate our bounty, that we not forget to reach out to the hungry and the poor. Give us compassionate hearts, loving God, alongside our grateful ones.

Help us reach out to all those who will be alone on Thanksgiving so that they will not be isolated on this special day. May our grateful hearts become generous hearts who long to include others who have no one with whom to celebrate.

For all those who worked to make our celebration a special one, we give thanks. For the bounty at our table and the ways you take care of us every day of our lives, we give thanks. Help us to never take for granted any of the special ways you bless us.

We thank you, Lord, for the love of our family and friends, and most especially your love, poured out to us in Christ Jesus. We pray that we may be signs of your love to all whom we meet.

We pray these things in the name of Jesus, your Son. Amen.

Prayers for
Following Jesus

Theological Virtues

Faith

Now faith is the assurance of things hoped for,
the conviction of things not seen.

Hebrews 11:1

Meditation: Jesus has a lot to say about faith in the Christian Scriptures. He tells us that if we have faith as small as a mustard seed we can move a mountain (Matthew 17:20), he chastises his disciple Peter for not having enough faith (Matthew 14:31) and he heals the daughter of a woman whose faith is great (Matthew 15:28). We receive the gift of faith through God's grace, and we strengthen our faith by practicing habits of right action.

Prayer: Loving God, you are the giver of all good things, and it is from you that we receive the gift of faith. Jesus tells us that "the one who believes in me will also do the works that I do" (John 14:12). Please strengthen our faith so we can continue Jesus' mission of healing, teaching, and loving others.

Bolster our confidence, Lord, when our faith falters, and show us that with you by our side, we have nothing to fear. Help us to witness our faith in you to others so they will know you are Lord of all.

We ask that you remind us of past occasions where you have responded to our need, loving God, so our faith for the future will be enhanced. Teach us to trust in your providence, Lord, when we find ourselves struggling in any way.

We ask that our faith may be a beacon of light to those who have lost their way, so that along with your guidance they may seek your truth. Though we do not know all the answers to life's questions, inspire us with your wisdom so that we can lead others to you.

All this we pray in the loving name of your Son and our Lord, Jesus. Amen.

Hope

For surely I know the plans I have for you, says the LORD,
plans for your welfare and not for harm,
to give you a future with hope.

Jeremiah 29:11

Meditation: God is intimately involved in our lives and desires wholeness and goodness for us. As human beings, however, we do not see the "big picture" as God does, and so we can become excruciatingly disappointed when we don't achieve the outcomes we want. In addition to trusting in God's providence, we need to be people of hope that God intends fullness of life for us.

Prayer: Jesus, as we continue to minister in your name, help us to witness to your unconditional love for your people. By our care for others, help us to be signs of hope to those who desperately need to know you never abandon those you love.

Give us enthusiasm and joy for our work so that we can be people of hope. Help us not to become bogged down by the tedious details of our jobs or by deadlines and pressures, but to remember that you are always by our side.

We pray for the gifts of vision and energy that we may see and respond to the needs of our time. Let us never be complacent in the face of suffering, but always willing to reach out as we are able.

May we recognize when our internal batteries need to be recharged and rejuvenated, so that we may never become bitter or burned out. Teach us the wisdom of self-care so that we can effectively respond to your call to care for others.

We especially ask that you instill hope for the future in our young people, who too often feel burdened by the world's problems they have inherited. We also lift up the needs of Mother Earth to you, Creator God, so that generations to come will have enough water, clean air, and resources to live.

This we pray in Jesus' name. Amen.

Love (Charity)

Love never ends. But as for prophecies, they will come to an end; as for tongues, they will cease; as for knowledge, it will come to an end. For we know only in part, and we prophesy only in part; but when the complete comes, the partial will come to an end.

1 Corinthians 13:8–107

Meditation: God, the author of all love, asks us to be loving toward one another. When we treat each other kindly and lovingly, we reflect God's love to each other. To truly love is at one time the easiest and yet the hardest thing to do, for love and forgiveness go hand in hand. As Jesus said, "Love your enemies, do good to those who hate you, bless those who curse you, pray for those who abuse you" (Luke 6:27–28).

Prayer: Loving God, by trying to answer your call to carry on the mission of Jesus, we are attempting to love in many different ways. When we feed the hungry, heal the sick, visit the prisoner or clothe the naked, we are fulfilling your invitation to love.

Give us the grace to love fully and unreservedly, knowing that our lives are short and our opportunities to give are finite. Help us not to put off until tomorrow the kindness we can do today. Remind us that even when we don't see the results of our caring, our efforts do make a difference.

Open us, Lord, to your love for us, that we may truly love other people. Through prayer and meditation, remind us of our status as your beloved children so we may never lose sight of our true identity.

May our love be a source of peace in a world too often rife with violence and hate.

This we ask in the name of your beloved Son, Jesus. Amen.

Cardinal Virtues

Prudence

All deeds are right in the sight of the doer, but the LORD
weighs the heart. To do righteousness and justice
is more acceptable to the LORD than sacrifice.

Proverbs 21:2–3

Meditation: When we are prudent, we apply our intellect to make a good decision. Oftentimes we need the advice of others to be truly prudent, as it can be difficult to be objective about our own situation. The Book of Proverbs makes a connection between wisdom and prudence, saying, "I, wisdom, live with prudence, and I attain knowledge and discretion" (Proverbs 8:12).

Prayer: God of wisdom, lead us in right ways so we may practice the virtue of prudence. We also ask that you place others in our path whose guidance we trust so our lives may be a reflection of you.

As we minister in your name, may the ventures we undergo be done with forethought and good judgment for the sake of your people. Help us to correct ourselves when we make mistakes and make right whatever wrongs we do.

Show us the importance of thinking before speaking and of knowing when to keep silent. In this world of instant gratification, help us to recognize that sometimes we need to slow down to hear your voice in our lives.

Jesus, you who taught with authority, place prudent leaders in our path whose right actions witness to your truth. Teach us to model good reasoning to our children, who need us to be examples of common sense so they can know security and well-being.

May we develop habits of discretion that lead to prudence, and may we always act with integrity and morality. We pray that we can learn from our past experiences so we can partner with you in creating a future with hope.

All this we pray in your loving name. Amen.

Justice

And what does the Lord require of you but to do justice,
and to love kindness, and to walk humbly with your God?

Micah 6:8

Meditation: Justice is one of the cardinal virtues, and is very important because it is built on the principle that we are created in the image and likeness of God, and so we should treat all persons with the dignity and respect they deserve. In 1972, Pope Paul VI said, "If you want peace, work for justice." People like Dorothy Day, Dr. Martin Luther King, Jr., Mahatma Gandhi, and Nelson Mandela were all models of what justice means because they sought to right the wrongs of the society in which they lived.

Prayer: Good and gracious God, teach us to be people of justice who long to do your will. Reveal to us the path upon which we should walk and help us to understand that your ways are not our ways.

Help us to be people of integrity who strive to do what is right. Inspire us with leaders who show us the meaning of ethical living and right relationship with others.

Forgive us for the times we do not behave justly and with compassion, and give us your grace so we may grow in the virtue of justice.

May we remember the times we have been treated unjustly so that we will not repeat others' unjust treatment, and help us to forgive those who have wronged us so that we don't inflict those same wrongs upon others.

Most importantly, Lord, let us grow in love toward all so that living justly becomes like second nature. We ask that we may always keep our eyes focused on your call to grow in the virtue of justice.

All this we pray in the name of your loving Son, Jesus. Amen.

Temperance (Restraint)

Do you not know that in a race the runners all compete, but only one receives the prize? Run in such a way that you may win it. Athletes exercise self-control in all things; they do it to receive a perishable wreathe, but we an imperishable one.

1 Corinthians 9:24–25

Meditation: Restraint, or temperance, is a virtue that is counter-cultural. We live in a society that promotes looking out for number one, and so we are encouraged to go after our desires and to not always consider the consequences of our actions. To practice restraint is to recognize we do not live in a vacuum; it also means that we see that the unbridled pursuit of our desires can have negative repercussions not only for ourselves but for others.

Prayer: Many of us have wounds from the past that make it difficult at times to say "no" to ourselves. We speak without thinking, we eat or drink too much, or we spend too much money.

Help us, Lord, to turn to you in times of temptation and know that you are all we need. With you by our side, loving God, we do not lack for anything, and all our wants are satisfied.

May we consider the feelings of others as much as we think about our own, and may we see that only with you are our deepest desires truly fulfilled. Help us to practice forgiveness when others do not consider our needs but act blindly without thinking about us.

In the Gospel of John, as Jesus was being arrested, he told Peter to put away his sword that had cut off the high priest's ear. Thus Jesus modeled to us the virtue of restraint at a very difficult moment in his life. We pray that we may always look to Jesus to see how we should act, especially at those times we need his guidance the most.

We pray this in his name. Amen.

Courage (Fortitude)

Do not fear, for I am with you, do not be afraid,
for I am your God; I will strengthen you, I will help you,
I will uphold you with my victorious right hand.

Isaiah 41:10

Meditation: It takes the cardinal virtue of courage to persevere in everyday life, for all of us face challenges of one sort or another. Sometimes our courage shows itself in quiet ways, like when we get up every morning to do the same thing day after day. But sometimes we are called upon to be courageous in big ways, as when Dr. Martin Luther King, Jr. boldly spoke out against racial injustice.

Prayer: Loving God, your Son, Jesus, demonstrated selfless courage in his desire to stand for love in the face of hatred. Our Christian tradition is filled with courageous martyrs who stood up for their faith, even to the point of dying for their beliefs. Help us to show courage in our daily lives so that we, too, can model this virtue to your people.

We thank you for the ways we see fortitude in the people to whom we minister: our students, patients, and parishioners. Oftentimes it is they who inspire us and not the other way around.

We ask for the grace to do the right thing, even when it is hard for us. Help us to recognize that sometimes courage and love go hand in hand, because it is not always easy to give of ourselves.

Give us fortitude, especially in our struggles, Lord, for that is when we need it the most. We pray for the ability to accept life's unavoidable burdens with humor and compassion, knowing that as we do so, we teach others to do the same.

We pray these things through Christ, our Lord. Amen.

Gifts of the Holy Spirit

Wisdom

Happy are those who find wisdom, and those who get understanding, for her income is better than silver, and her revenue better than gold.

Proverbs 3:13–14

Meditation: The gift of wisdom helps us make good choices throughout our lives, and as such it is a very valuable gift. We receive wisdom by our baptism, but it can also be enhanced and strengthened by life's experiences and by maturity. The Book of Proverbs tells us that "those who hold [wisdom] fast are called happy" (Proverbs 3:18).

Prayer: Loving God, we thank you for the gift of wisdom we receive through your Holy Spirit. You are a God who longs to bless us abundantly with your grace, and we praise and honor you.

May we always be mindful that without your wisdom, we are nothing. Help us to also remember that through our ministry, we are called to be examples of your wisdom to the people we serve.

Put into our paths those wise men and women whose guidance lights our way and illumines our choices. Give us the humility to always seek after your wisdom when we struggle for answers to our questions.

May we never lead astray those whose care you have entrusted to us. Help us especially to look after our children and those who are weak and vulnerable. May we always seek forgiveness for our rash decisions and the times we have not waited for your direction.

True wisdom enables us to live in harmony with our resources rather than seeking dominion over them. Help us to make wise choices regarding the future of our earth so we may conserve its treasures for generations to come.

We thank you for the beloved figures of wisdom in our own lives, especially our grandparents and all our elders who teach us by their experience.

We pray these things through Christ, our Lord. Amen.

Understanding

*If you indeed cry out for insight, and raise your voice for
understanding; if you seek it like silver, and search for it
as for hidden treasures—then you will understand
the fear of the LORD and find the knowledge of God.*

Proverbs 2:3–5

Meditation: Understanding is the second gift of the Holy Spirit, and is an example of God's life within us. Scripture is full of illustrations of how God's ways are not our ways. When we receive the gift of understanding by grace, we have a renewed vision, a different way of seeing ourselves, others and the world than we did before. We cannot arrive at understanding through our own will, but we can open ourselves to receiving this gift.

Prayer: O God, you are the giver of all good gifts, and we thank you and praise you. Instill in us the gift of understanding so we may come closer to the truths of the universe and learn more how to walk in your ways.

May we yearn to see as you see not for our own glory, but so that we may help those you have called us to serve. May our understanding we receive from you lead us to greater compassion and forgiveness of all with whom we come in contact.

Please remove the barriers to our understanding, and forgive us for those times we refuse to accept the gifts you wish to offer us. We pray that through the grace of your Holy Spirit, we may be signs of your understanding to the world.

Many live in ignorance of your love for us, O God, and we pray that as we grow in understanding of you, we may also witness to others your tenderness toward all. We thank you for always wanting what is best for us.

All this we pray in the loving name of Jesus, your Son and our Lord. Amen.

Counsel

Indeed, the word of God is living and active,
sharper than any two-edged sword, piercing
until it divides soul from spirit, joints from marrow;
it is able to judge the thoughts and intentions of the heart.

Hebrews 4:12

Meditation: Sometimes we are called upon to make decisions quickly, with little opportunity for forethought. Perhaps a loved one is acutely ill and we need to decide upon an emergency treatment for that person. Or maybe a job opportunity presents itself to us suddenly and there is not much time to deliberate. When situations like these arise, the Holy Spirit gives us the gift of counsel to help us choose rightly which course of action to take.

Prayer: Spirit of wisdom and understanding, we live in a fast-paced world where the needs of others are constantly changing. Give us the gift of counsel to know how to best respond to your people as you would have us do.

Many are the voices competing for our attention, and sometimes our internal clamor from our busy lives threatens to keep us from the still, small voice of your Spirit within. But you, God, are a patient and persistent God, and we trust you to always lead us rightly if we just ask for your help.

Be with our young people in a special way, loving God, as they need your counsel perhaps more than anyone else to navigate the journey of growing up in this complicated world.

Help us to be a guiding light for others, Lord, when they turn to us for help, and may we always seek your input so that we may be able to advise them truly. When we ourselves stumble and fall in our efforts to follow you, give us the grace to forgive ourselves and move forward.

All this we pray in the name of your Son Jesus, our Lord. Amen.

Fortitude

When they bring you before the synagogues, the rulers,
and the authorities, do not worry about how to defend yourselves
or what you are to say; for the Holy Spirit will teach you
at that very hour what you ought to say.

Luke 12:11–12

Meditation: Fortitude is not only a cardinal virtue but also a gift of the Holy Spirit. The gift of fortitude allows us to stand up for what is right, even in the face of opposition, and sometimes even to the point of dying for our beliefs. People like Dr. Martin Luther King, Jr., Mahatma Gandhi, and Dietrich Bonhoeffer were all endowed with the gift of fortitude. Fortitude can also enable us to face adversity and loss with dignity and grace.

Prayer: Every day, Lord, we are faced with challenges as we attempt to minister in your name, and we need your grace to withstand our daily difficulties. Holy Spirit, give us the gift of fortitude that we might be persons of honor no matter what comes our way.

Help us to be shining examples of what it means to be a Christian in this day and age, when greed, dishonesty, and disillusionment seem to be prevalent. We ask that we be especially mindful of the people around us who display the gift of fortitude, some of whom are ordinary people with extraordinary callings.

Holy Spirit, we pray for the gift of fortitude to help us bear our crosses—those infirmities and losses that seem unbearable at times. We know that nothing is impossible with you, Lord, and we thank you for sustaining us in our trials.

Give us the strength, Lord, not to seek the easy way out when we are threatened with troublesome times, but to always look to you for guidance and help.

All this we pray in the name of Jesus, our Lord. Amen.

Knowledge

For we know only in part, and we prophecy only in part;
but when the complete comes, the partial will come to an end....
Now I know only in part; then I will know fully,
even as I have been fully known.

1 Corinthians 13:9–10, 12

Meditation: Those of us who have a trusted ally, a friend we can turn to when we need sound advice, are fortunate indeed. Guidance from the Holy Spirit is always available to us, however, when we quietly open ourselves to receive the gift of knowledge. Our lives begin to take on a rhythm and balance when we act upon the promptings of the Spirit in our minds and in our hearts.

Prayer: Holy Spirit, you are the font of all wisdom and knowledge, and it is you we turn to for guidance in the activities of our daily lives. Through the gift of your knowledge, teach us the ability to discern rightly whenever we are faced with an important decision.

Give us the grace to sift through the inner stirrings of our hearts so we can discover the truth that comes from you. Lead us to seek out those people and places who foster our spiritual growth so we may be encouraged in our journey toward wholeness.

Spirit of knowledge, we ask that we not be overly discouraged by our mistakes, but that you help us pick ourselves up, shake ourselves off, and start again.

May our choices always be made in love as we learn how to best serve your people. May we look to you, Holy Spirit, as we seek out new ways to continue the mission of Jesus in our world. Thank you for showing us where we are needed most in our ministry.

All this we pray in the name of our Savior, Jesus Christ. Amen.

Piety

*Finally, beloved, whatever is true, whatever is honorable,
whatever is just, whatever is pure, whatever is pleasing,
whatever is commendable, if there is any excellence and
if there is anything worthy of praise, think about these things.*

Philippians 4:8

Meditation: For some people, being good seems to be second nature. For others, being and doing good takes more of an effort. The important thing to remember is that God, the giver of all good gifts, transforms us by grace, and instills in us the desire to do good. This desire or motivation to do good is called piety, the sixth gift of the Holy Spirit. "For I am the LORD your God; sanctify yourselves therefore, and be holy, for I am holy" (Leviticus 11:44).

Prayer: Source of all goodness, you call us to be in relationship to you. You tell us in Leviticus 26:12 that "I will walk among you, and will be your God, and you shall be my people."

We thank you, God, for the new life in Christ that we receive by virtue of our baptism. As we recognize our new status as your beloved sons and daughters, help us to always stay focused on you as we open ourselves to receive the gift of piety.

Help us to see, God, that your invitation to holiness calls us to direct our attention outward. Many are the needs of your people, Lord: they cry out for help all over the globe. Stir our hearts with your compassion, and renew in us our commitment to serve others.

Loving God, your call to conversion is lifelong and requires that we dedicate our whole beings to you and only you. Give us the grace to let go of that which stands in the way of responding wholeheartedly to you, and help us to embrace all that brings us closer to you.

All this we pray in the name of your Son, Jesus, our Lord. Amen.

Fear of the Lord

Teach me your way, O LORD, that I may walk in your truth;
give me an undivided heart to revere your name.
I give thanks to you, O Lord my God, with my whole heart,
and I will glorify your name for ever.

Psalm 86:11–12

Meditation: When we love someone, we go to great lengths not to hurt that person or disrupt that relationship, and this is true of our relationship with God as well. Fear of the Lord means we desire to maintain our closeness with God and that we recognize our dependence on the Lord. It also means that we respect and revere God, for we realize that God is perfect. "The fear of the Lord is the beginning of wisdom" (Psalm 111:10).

Prayer: God of glory and majesty, we come before you today with humble hearts, for we know that you provide everything good in our lives. We thank you that you have called us to minister, in love, to your people in this day and age.

Help us to recognize that our work is not about us but about you, and that we can do nothing without you. We pray that we may always turn to you for the strength to continue Jesus' mission of healing, preaching, and teaching.

You are the Alpha and the Omega, the beginning and the end, and all creation sings your praise. Until the day comes that we see you face to face, be the hope that guides us and the power that sustains us throughout our lives.

We ask forgiveness for the times we have ignored your invitation to be the hands and feet of Christ to those who suffer. We seek clarity on how best to respond to the needs of our time so we may be instruments of your healing presence.

We pray these things through Christ, our Lord. Amen.

About the Author

Sally Macke has more than twenty years of experience as a hospital chaplain in the St. Louis area. She holds a master's degree in pastoral studies and a certificate in spiritual direction from Aquinas Institute of Theology in St. Louis. Sally is a board-certified chaplain through the Association of Professional Chaplains, and she currently ministers in the intensive-care units of Mercy Hospital St. Louis. Sally also trains new leaders for Mercy's East Region in how to lead prayer. She is the author of *Prayers for Healing Body and Soul*, published by Liguori Publications.

CPSIA information can be obtained at www.ICGtesting.com
Printed in the USA
LVOW05s1157131114

413492LV00005B/8/P